Redshift

4

ARROYO SECO PRESS

Arroyo Seco Press

Redshift Anthology #4

Edited by Kevin Ridgeway

www.arroyosecopress.org
www.redshiftmag.org

logo by Morgan G. Robles
morganrobles.carbonmade.com

Cover image: iStock sololos & Pathlord

ISBN-13: 978-1-7326911-3-1
ISBN-10: 1-7326911-3-4

for Michelle

Poems

Redshift

sail the moon
silent on solar winds
dancing dreams

Matt Amott

Terminal Philosophy

I have nowhere else to go,
so I arrive
at the airport
hours before
my flight.
Sitting there
watching the people
come and go
is when I realize
that whether the breakup
was her fault or mine,
life goes on.

Matt Amott

Broad Strokes

She needed to get away
so she booked a trip.
Three weeks traveling
around the Mediterranean,
experiencing the people
and culture
of ancient cities
and coastal towns
with buildings in bright
orange, yellows and pinks.
Villages with sidewalks
white like the sand
whose stucco houses are splashed
in the same blue that reflects
off the nearby sea.

I was little surprised
that she came home
but she said
she didn't want to
start a new life
over there,
she just wanted to
bring back some color
to her life here.

Mark James Andrews

Isn't It Good?

I parked & launched out of my Corvair
just about 8 Miles High at my girlfriend's house
she of the ginger hair & grey eyes.
I called her Bridge.

Bridge was having a party for her little sister
& a big gaggle of teeny bop girls
some picked for the May crowning ceremony
at Holy Name of Jesus church

a Roman Catholic throwback pagan ceremony
a Celtic flower gathering & May Pole disguise.
The crowner girls were dangerously sexed up.

Bridge's sister would soon climb a dais
at the side altar & crown the Madonna with flowers
above vigil candles in red glass cups flickering.

There was a group of long-hair boys standing
on the curb out front smoking cigarettes.
One of them flipped his butt
& stepped forward toward me.

"Hey man, you got any chemicals?"
"What do I look like a scientist?
Get the fuck out of here."

Mark James Andrews

I could hear the organ of Born to Be Wild
from the backyard & moved through the front gate
on the side of the house & walked through
the dark skinny tunnel between houses.

There were no driveways on Bridge's block.
& the lots were small.
I came out of the tunnel into
a department store Christmas display.

There were strings of color Christmas lights
weaved on the clotheslines
& plastic Nativity figures
in the middle of the yard

with the Virgin Mary front & center
on a thin wooden slat bushel basket
with a crown of blue plastic posies.
mounted on her head.

There was a break in the music.
Then a scratchy sounding 45 RPM
of My Girl dropped on the turntable.

Bridge was running back and forth
getting the kids to slow dance
to the Temptations.

Mark James Andrews

Then she saw me and walked over.
She had on my favorite dress
"the get naked dress."

"These kids are so cute.
Look at them."

"Yeah. But the drug addicts
are hanging tough out front."

"Well, I guess you belong
out front with them."

& so I lit a fire for a weenie roast
in a rusty tripod barbecue
& thought isn't it good?

firstborn of the dead

how could I forget the way
you wobbled in high heels
the way you chewed your hair
when you were nervous
which may have been all the time
the way you looked in that black skirt
even with your legs covered in bruises
you had the best ass I've ever seen

I remember the day
we stole your dads
'78 Cutlass Supreme
he spent the last year refurbishing
he just put the for sale sign in the window

we chewed off the back roads
left it after it ran out of gas
walked forever junk sick
to a wal mart, scored
a ride back to town
your dad never suspected
or you never let me know

Jason Baldinger

honestly, I can't remember all the funerals
on bad nights when there's a new moon
when the stars are wound in sheets
they all come back. I know I lost track
of you and don't know if you're
somewhere in the world, or gone
maybe it's easier if I believe you're gone

I feel like the next line is the summation
of a dream, but I kicked heroin, knocked up my best
girl, got fat, moved to a town big enough
to have a stop light, a post office and a cult
maybe that's all that's left

firstborn of the dead
found nights gazing at stars
wondering where the intersection
is between the sweet life and eternity

7

Jason Baldinger

tripping into sunrise

it was a five am thing
couple days a week
his frizzy hair in half-light
parka and a bicycle
through suburban highways
walking through the door
always asking the same thing
did you get any new light bulbs?

we spent lunch hours
lighting farts on fire
this behavior not as odd
as this man, who
for the next hour
sniffed every lightbulb
until we pulled pallets away
leaving the high
that mercury or argon
or whatever fucking chemical
had, harvested another day

polite, he'd thank us
stumbled out the door
back to his bike, poisoned
tripping into the sunrise

Luis Cuauhtémoc Berriozábal

Sea Song Agonies

The sea wants to sing
its agonies, in the
language of waves,
and shipwrecked vessels.

How it wants to spread
its song on dry land,
drop saltwater on fresh
flowers and dying grass.

How it wants to sing in
blood, for all the drowned
sailors and the babes
who never learned to swim.

Luis Cuauhtémoc Berriozábal

Night Winds

The candle burns
and night sleeps

without dreaming.

Like a black cat
licking its feet,
night winds caress
the homeless who

think of their next
meal in their dreams
at day or night.

Flight Plan

The painter's frock catches the light as they paint
trajectory of falling colors, sunsetting off cliff,
I too stare out over the edge of things—it is low tide,
marine layer misty above barely visible Channel Islands
from here, I have watched a child climb up the face of it.
The child forgetting her kite, laughs

Her dress a sail, she catches the air, and the sky
in all its depth unfolds between us—I am rooted.
She is the child I want. She is a sky for dreaming
untold. Sand between my toes crinkles. A peregrine
falcon back from the brink of extinction hovers, vents
off the same breeze propelling the girl. The perfect kite.

I want to go around giving us all a slice of cake,
but my hands make mush of it. I'm convinced anyways
that pie is better, makes the jazz behind my knees
wiggle just a little, like maybe I've missed a beat or two,
but I don't have that either pie   cake

I realize the jukebox has been stuck on the same song,
needs an errant kick and that I need a break in the loop,
but I didn't choose what's been broken, so can only offer
this fix, I open my hands like duct tape, knowing
of course, that this is the solution 99% of the time

Kelsey Bryan-Zwick

As the child lands, reeled in on her miniscule thread, I save
the pie for another day. Dream of other cake. Give her a pair
of makeshift wings knowing soon she'll be untethered, a jar
of honey for the journey, and I only point out the ocean, the sun.

Kelsey Bryan-Zwick

Scrambled Eggs

The commercial circa the 90s, you may
remember, smashes the whole egg with
a frying pan. Says, *This is your brain
on drugs!* The dripping mess of it all over
kitchen and I am freaked out, freaking out
all eleven years of me and post-op
my poor brain, I think, *how it will suffer*
as I swallow the pills the doctors prescribe
remember the morphine drip, but with
such a smashed-up brain I begin to wonder
if what I am is remembering at all, *my
cracked shell, my oozing.*

Kelsey Bryan-Zwick

Clutched in my Fist the Bag I Carry
—after Tim O'Brien's short story, "The Things They Carried."

Carries keys to car, front door, small room with bed
stash of meds to swallow, chapstick that wets the lips
sunglasses that cut the California glare, matches—

Or a light, the wallet that says: who, what, when, where
and how much, a phone: fishing line tied to photos and friends
voicemail, text, ink pen, square of paper, a borrowed book—

Packet of tissue, which serves as emergency sanitary napkin
stuffing for the unfulfilled bra, stuffing open-ended wounds
soaking up the tears, plugging up bloodied bent noses—

Blotting watercolor sunsets, un-smudging blurred lines
leaving him dear John note, or to get the next number, recipe
favorite quote, muffling ears because the yelling won't stop—

Anxious folding origami animals, sopping up the spilled
    everything
flammable enough to stuff the Molotov cocktail, or dampen with
water to cover mouth, the only way forward is through the fire—

The Boys Come

Slumming
out of Kirkwood
back in the day.

When they came across Gert,
they got lucky.
When they came across me,
they got stiches,
a trip to emergency,
broken, busted up
like they needed
a lesson.
I took them to a spot
where My Boys would be.

I know a spot
over here
come this way, baby

-it's not true-

They never came
slumming
because they were too good
                    for that.

Ranney Campbell

My Boys didn't protect me.
They were after me.
My Boys needed a beating
            and they got one.
Not from me,
But because it was inevitable.

Misses Risotto

carnoroli
riso
superfino
served with scallops tonight
made with mushrooms
for your wife
with seafood stock
  olive
oil
spanish onion finely chopped
add pinot, sneak some
taste on your tongue
while you tend
the broth and you stir inside
rice swell release starchy creaming
salty pinch turn pepper cranking
as she enters from her little
mindless job
that kept her away

two eat together bind
over eons of evolved autonomic pairing same inside as
running
fingers through thick dark hair

Ranney Campbell

to stay halfway
alive while dead safe

grasping for imaginary others
while again eating your surrogate
neutered passion

Ranney Campbell

Pimp

More important to stretch my leg over my head the best I can
while lying on my back on my bed than to read another
introduction written by Jeffers of one of his books of poetry
even though I think his words touching because what would
be more important than to be quite limber just in case you
ever decide to go through with any one of those threats you
make to fuck me, pimp?

I held my left leg
about ninety degrees

remembered when
way back in the nineties
I could lay it down
next to my ear.

Todd Cirillo

High School Reunion

At the beach bar
as far south as the road can go,
a song
from my high school years
comes on the jukebox—
"The Heart of the Matter"
by Don Henley.
It played on MTV,
at slow dances,
under bedroom black lights,
on poster plastered walls,
in the front seat of cars,
behind buildings,
at low lit dead ends.

To get this far away,
all these miles,
moments
and years
spent mostly
on barstools
around the world—

Todd Cirillo

a very long, long way
from those dirt road days
living in a hated town
full of rotten apple orchards,
run-down bowling alleys,
an annual peach festival
that everyone talked about year-round,
cornfield drinking,
all those confused first fumblings at love…

only to end up back here again,
fucked up with my loneliness,
sitting on an old wooden barstool
with long gone names carved into it,
in the sunshine and sweet breeze—

just another one of the boys of summer
who tried to get away.

There is No Story Here

      Balance
in our minds   that shape
   we speak it into being
believe

that everything has a story
that there is no beauty
until someone
beholds it   names it

Foolish—

      Wanting
a finger's width
of some   one thing
   freshly birthed
unshaped by opinion
an outsider   untouched
by the senses

Just—

And, Yet, They Hold
—*after reading Rachel Carson*

Tenacious lives
are lived along tide lines;
mussels, periwinkles, limpets.
They cling; a single foot planted,
or a shell glued
against the ferocity
of gathered depths that slam
every day into rockweed,
into bladder wrack. Then always,
the great sucking retreat—
tearing and tugging. And, yet, they hold.

I have known the grasp of water.
Have felt the relentless weight of sky.
Have driven my two good feet, bleeding,
down paths that divide and divide again
until only a sliver of myself remains.
Now, balanced on this bubbled mat
of kelp and rockweed, I willingly swallow
this acrid air—this ancient salt.

For here in the wrack one does not falter.
In the oceanic push and pull of tides
are many lives. They have held on—
are holding, yet.

Shutta Crum

On the Beach

Boys in sea-soaked swim trunks
skim rocks across the waves. A few skip,
then sink resolutely after
having spent centuries rolling in the surf,
smoothing edges, destroying evidence
of ancient algae, reptile tread, soot-filled skies.

They've come to rest on this beach.
Here, where summer-reddened boys
bend over them, studiously selecting,
turning each over and over in the ancestral
salt that wells up from the palms of their hands.

It's a small betrayal—
before drooping trunks are pulled up,
legs are braced and eyes squeezed
to squint across the unknown deep.
Played out with a simple side-arm fling,
each stone returning to the endless churn.

By my foot, a teardrop of pink granite
infinitely old, deliberately worn, wise.
I put it in my pocket.

John Dorsey

Every Year at the Children's Hospital

i'd be filled with dread
having to spend all day
in a waiting room
with other disabled kids
just so a doctor could test my reflexes
& ask me about my day
on an uncomfortable metal table

after more than forty years
it hasn't gotten any better
i still break out in hives
at the thought of having to find parking
in downtown pittsburgh
just thinking about the garage
that my dad would always
have to remember
to bring enough change for

i'm not an animal
tables were made for dinner
& polite conversation
not for sitting on
no matter how great
your day was.

John Dorsey

Color Theory in the Summer of 1980

on the news all they talked about was the hostage crisis
ronald reagan looked like john wayne
with whiter teeth or the ghost of gig young
coming back to bring our boys home
from the past

i drank donald duck grapefruit juice
& made war with plastic army men
on our green shag carpet almost every night
until the sun went down

we always freed the hostages
we always waved the flag
unless i got sleepy

like one night
when i spilled juice
all over the tv

red
white
&
blue

suddenly became blue & green bars
on every channel

my father refused to replace it
for at least 10 years

it was perfectly good

by then the hostages really were free
& my men were buried in the backyard
or taken away in garbage bags

the summer sun was sticky
& blood was the color
it was always
supposed to be.

John Drudge

Scattering

And at the end
Of the tattered tail
Provoked by desire
But denied the experience
The frustrations
Of a youthful song
That sings in the winds
Beyond our reasoning
And the addiction
To our suffering
That afflicts
The pattern of our
Ebbing voltage
Disappearing
Into the scattered winter
Of voices
Weeping

James H Duncan

Derelict

1. a dismal sort of distance
not unlike that between the dirt road
and the one shoe
lying sideways
out there in the farmer's field,
the cut cornstalks looking like transient stubble,
like arrows fired down from the sky
surrounding the leather castaway,
laces frayed
and flickering in the wind
laces streaming across no-man-land,
grayscale disillusionment,
and dead crops that
even time cannot bring back

2. the last of my things
are in a box in the kitchen, she said,
and it would be best if I got them
when she wasn't there,
one of the few things we agreed on
in those final days, and so
my feet echoed through the living room,
the dining room, the hall,

James H Duncan

everything empty, the years packed away
and gone, and my one
last box there on the counter,
beside it the glint of sunlight appearing
through a scarred silver ring
the one I left behind, now left behind for good
sitting on green formica where not even
the desire to exchange it for cash
was a strong enough feeling to keep it dear,
and there it remained
when I closed the door and walked
down the street to my car,
a promise embraced by hollow rooms
and dust motes drifting in the setting sun

3. a car leaving nothing but dust and detritus
under the setting sun, the silver moon,
the silent edge of town painted
in grayscale disillusionment

dead crops that
even time cannot bring back

Barbara Eknoian

My Saudade

I'm enjoying a massage,
while "A Summer Place"
plays in the background.
It triggers memories
from my teen years at the lake.
I see his blond hair, his smile,
his broad shoulders.
I recall my strong crush on Ronnie.
I missed him once before
when he came looking for me,
and missed him again
when he joined the Navy
on the first day I returned
to the lake the next summer
My massage continues.
I imagine what might have been:
he pulls up to the dock,
asks me to go for a ride
in his speedboat.
I hop in and we head
for the River Styx Bridge.
The boat bangs up and down
against choppy waves
and wind messes my hair,
but I don't care.
I'm in love again.
I don't want my massage to end.

Saudade, a deep emotional state of nostalgic longing

Barbara Eknoian

Café de Paree

I am sixteen on vacation in Miami.
My mom and her two friends
take me out to Café de Paree.
The show highlights fiery red-haired
Tempest Storm,
who slinks on the stage
in a black sequin gown.
pausing to peel off long white gloves.

Finally, she's down to a G-string
and wears pasties with tassels
on her breasts.
I'm fascinated wondering how
she could get them to twirl
first to the right and then to the left.

I look up twirling tassels on Google
and see a tutorial by Red Hot Annie
who instructs:
one has to shimmy, pump the shoulders,
bounce lightly on toes,
to make them twirl in one direction,
raise one arm up over head and point.

For a challenging move, so that only
one tassel rotates, press one arm
close to the body and shrug,
pump up and shrug.
Then she bounces, lifts up one arm
over her head to reverse the rotation

Now, I'm not sure why I looked up
these twirling tassels' instructions.
Maybe, for use in my next life?

Barbara Eknoian

Wanderer

In the shabby light of your hospital room
non-stop videos transport you
to prairies, mountains, a yacht off
of Monte Carlo, imagining the comfort
of a woman by your side, the feel of her breath
on your neck, a blanket shared, her perfume.

You were the happy wanderer at Woodstock
with your hippie friends, free to smoke weed,
and philosophize about life.
Then you crossed country to meet a pen pal
in Iowa, where you often supped at "Sally's Place,"
the Salvation Army's kitchen.
When things got too crazy there, you traveled
to California, interned as a barber, danced
on Saturday nights at a country western bar.
Your Woodstock buddies called pulling you back
to the woods, the tall trees, the rippling streams.
Then another town, pen pal, or family issue
drew you like a magnet. Couldn't stay put.

Now in your hospital bed, ailing with AIDS,
you have hours and hours to ponder.
You say, I made a big mistake.
I should've stayed with Betty and the girls.
I was too young for marriage.
And I really miss Daddy, I loved him.

Alexis Rhone Fancher

Midnight In The Backyard of Lust and Longing

The sapphists are at it again. *Screw you's!* ricochet off our common walls, invectives landmine my window. *You cheating bitch!* Like clockwork, this drunken Friday night climax to their ceaseless lovers' quarrel. *I'll kill you!* I hear the big one growl. And then the smashed plates, the screams. By the time the cops arrive it's a full-out brawl, the two women spilling from their back door, tussling across the no man's land between their tiny backyard and mine. Worse than animals. This time it's Holly, the younger one, dragged to the patrol car, yellow hair wilding, small hands cuffed behind her back, kicking at the cops in those *Daisy Dukes*, an army jacket waifing her silhouette. More clothes than she had on the last time the cops rolled up. Or the time before. It's almost dawn, and the trees shiver in the fog, raccoons slink through the tall grass. Marie, Holly's better half, paces the yard in a blue bathrobe and slippers, smoking a cigarette, sobbing as the cops jam her lover into their car. *Watch her head!* she cries, and flings herself across the yard, lunges for Holly through the glass. *Baby! Baby!* she sobs, the reason for their discord forgotten. Holly mouths a sloppy kiss. Marie opens her robe, presses herself against the glass. Can you believe it? I would give anything to be loved like that.

Alexis Rhone Fancher

She Says Stalker/He Says Fan
— "If you can't be free, be a mystery." - Rita Dove, 'Canary.'

She's a singed torch song, a broken chord, the slip-shadow between superstar and the door. She's that long stretch of longing riding shotgun from nowhere to L.A., a bottle of Jack Daniels snug between her thighs, always some fresh loser at the wheel. She's the Zippo in your darkness, a glimmer of goddess in your god-forsaken life, her voice a rasp, a whisky-tinged caress. She *gets* you, and you know the words to all her songs, follow her from dive bar to third-rate club clapping too loudly, making sure she makes it home. She's as luckless in love as you are, star-crossed, the pair of you, (in your dreams). If only we could choose who we love! Tonight the bartender pours your obsession one on the house, dims the lights in the half-empty room as she walks on stage, defenseless, but for that 0018 rosewood Martin she cradles in her lap like a child. If you ask nicely, she'll end with the song you request night after night, about the perils of unrequited love. You'll blurt out your worship into her deaf ear, while her fingers strum your forearm and her nails break your skin. *Give the lady whatever she wants,* you'll tell the barkeep. Like that's even possible.

Scott Ferry

I cut open

a pomegranate quickly,
slice down the too-white flesh
with my smallest

sharpest blade,
trace the partitions of skin
all the way down the body,

pull open the lungs
with some skill
to prevent further bleeding.

I only have five minutes
and blood blooms onto
every clean surface—

my hands, my scrubs,
my forearms. Arils
tumble into the bowl—

wet larynges, ripped
pericardial sacs, broken
fists. I taste one

and it is just sweet enough
to serve to my daughter.
I seal the plastic lid

so that no air
escapes.

Scott Ferry

Sandstone (1995)

This is not the first time I have hiked up this firebreak
between buckwheat and wishbone and California fescue
to the cement sheds and tilting antennae at the spine
of these hills. But it is dusk, I have no flashlight,
and I have ingested a full hit of LSD. I don't know why

I thought it was a good idea to take the acid, much less
hike up the veins of dust barely visible through
scrub oak and sycamore in near darkness.
Truth is, I need to break up with my girlfriend
because I don't find her physically attractive.

Maybe I never did. I love her because she is the hippy
I can never commit to being and her glow smears my eyes
with light. I am also quitting teaching only after 2 years
because I not only can't control the beings
in my continuation school classes,

I don't want to. I want them to be interested
in anything: Elie Wiesel, George Orwell,
Alicia Partnoy, Joy Harjo. I bleed myself out
reading to them. I hope some listen, I can't tell.
I whistle with wind. I realize I'm not the person

for this work, or that I'm not able to be that person.
Also, I have begun seeing auras and my sense of
reality flickers like the lights of the tractors in the valley
scraping off the skin of the Laguna hills to create
a toll road. I sit on a scapula of sandstone and weep.

It is not advisable to cry while on a heavy hallucinogenic
because the crying rips out laurel and wax myrtle
and lilac with pneumatic claws. And a blackness
burrows through femur though ilium through sternum
until the sky is a breath of ashen seeds.

I don't know how long I wail—
blue bones, opal marrow, spit and dry calls
to distant gears tearing at the nerves. But
when I walk back down the mount,
I know what has to be done.

Nephomancy: by clouds

I used to dream of walking into them
by climbing up my cement wall.
I didn't know what I would do there,
I was five. I just knew there
could be a place without yelling,
or sirens, or people. Maybe I
just wanted a place without
people. Or just the best parts
of the people I loved.
The tuck in at night, the tacos
and the ice cream, the laughing
at the same book, the holding
me in their arms. Maybe we
could be like that there, I thought.
Weightless, like the air inside
balloons.

Michael Flanagan

Curfew

We sat on the porch of the rehab
talking after lights out, breaking
curfew like junkies will, summer
air worth something there
in the leafy suburbs, far from
the city streets we'd both come
close to dying on. Two desperate
hearts, rags for souls, laughing
at how good it felt to break a rule,
Tony lighting a last cigarette, telling
me about the work he'd left,
the number of jobs laying tile
waiting, or not waiting, for his
return, how he'd been running
the damn business into the ground
anyway, the overnight councilor,
John, coming outside eventually,
wanting to know what we thought
we were doing. The two of ya',
he growled, can't help yourselves,
can ya'. Tony told him last smoke
and an hour went by, John laying hard
dark truths on us, tapping me
on the shoulder at one point,

Michael Flanagan

the taps getting sharper after each
one, finally John saying, it's like
that, the small things nagging you
until you break, taking the annoyance
as reason to use again. At the top
of the stairs, heading to our beds,
Tony and I hugged. Damn, we both
said, awed by the magic of all that
had been laid on us, wisdom we
felt we would always hold,
both of us walking out weeks later,
cocksure after our months stay,
only to use again immediately, years
later, clean finally, never having
forgotten. And Tony. Out of my life
forever. Not a surprise if I heard he'd
overdosed ages ago, or crawled finally
to sanity, either outcome as likely
for him as it had long been for me.

Michael Flanagan

Pathos

How many times can a person re-direct a mentally
challenged adult to a better way of socializing, only
to watch them repeat the same misguided behaviors
hour after hour. How many times can you fill out
the same report, be assaulted by the same client,
the hectic eight hours like ground hog day on speed,
grown babies screaming for bottles, wanting diapers
changed, Monday turning into Friday, months into
years. At home I lie on the couch, sleep a quick half
hour, get up, sit at a desk, try to write a decent line,
tell a story, sing a poem. Exhausted I last ten minutes,
maybe an hour. People often say, on your death bed,
though you hadn't known it, you realize you've
ended up having gained the things that actually
fill you. I talked to a geriatric nurse once though.
She said just as often, the dying are bitter,
remain disillusioned, feel they've missed by miles,
or inches, either measurement enough to make
it all seem worthless. Recently I was diagnosed
with high blood pressure. I changed my diet,
take the medication. I'm fifty years into this
and that fucking clock is ticking so loud my ears
are screaming. I know this poem is a waste
of time. It tells the truth but lacks pathos. When
I take to this chair next time I promise to search
for something like water released from gravity,
rushing across miles of sky. Perhaps I'll stumble
on a star broken into pieces, burning in the wide
open, by an ocean with blue waves crashing.

Bill Gainer

Needing Wishes

The wish —
a delicate wrist
small, thin
one deserving
of its own
fragrance
and silver bangles —
worn late
into the morning.
Let them jingle
when she wakes.
There are other things
needing wishes
too.
We'll just start here.
Move on later.

Bill Gainer

Different Kinds of Friends

I've seen a horse's face
in the leaves of a tree…
between the blinds
peeking out
a hot
end of summer
day.
Other things
too.
Real and imaginary.

I don't respond
to the neighbor's screams
anymore.
She's given me a code
word, for help.
I didn't tell her
I hear things too.
Real and imaginary.

It's been happening
a while now.
I don't talk about it much.

Bill Gainer

If the wrong people
find out
they might want to
take my:
driver's license
pistol
and kitchen knives
away.

Or even
try to cure me
of the problem.

If it is
a problem.
I wouldn't like that.
It's nice not being
lonely.
It only scares me
sometimes.

Tony Gloeggler

Daylight Savings

When I climb out
of the subway, the sun
still sits in the sky. I take
the long way home, cut
through the park. Boom
boxes beat hip hop
and the basketball courts
are jammed with brothers
running full out. I curl
my fingers around fence
links, taste sweat
wetting my lips, whisper
"I got next." Girls straddle
benches, stand in circles
waving cigarettes, heads
flung back, flicking smoke
signals. A grandfather
underhands a fat wiffle ball.
The little kid swings, hits
a humpbacked fly. I trot
a few steps, catch it
over my shoulder like Mays
in '54. I grab a slice
with extra cheese. Squeeze
melons, mangos, nectarines.

Tony Gloeggler

Pick up laundry and unlock
my mail box. Home. One
more hour of light to kill
remembering my father died
February first, that the last
time I slept with a woman
was nearly seven months ago
in Corrales, New Mexico
and I didn't love
one thing about her.

Tony Gloeggler

Poet

The first time anyone
said my name and used
the word poet next to it
was in the early nineties.
I was part of William Packard's
workshop and after class
he told me about this reading
celebrating New York Quarterly's
30th anniversary. He declared
in his booming Orson Wells voice
that I would read one poem
and even if he badly needed
a shower with seven vestal
virgins scrubbing away, I knew
I couldn't, wouldn't say no.

I dressed in my best black jeans
and faded denim shirt, found
the room in the NYU library
and pointed at my name
on the flyer when the pristine
woman at the door asked me
for 10 dollars. I would read
somewhere in the middle,
between Michael Moriarty
and Amari Baraka and already

Tony Gloeggler

I was nervous, trying to sneak
glances at the spiral notepaper
my poem was scribbled on.

Moriarity read in the voice
he saved for Shakespeare
or the sermon on the mount
and I expected the cheese
and crackers to turn into steak
and lobster. No, I can't say
I understood what his poem
was trying to be about, but back
home I started watching Law
and Order religiously. Baraka's
spit flew through his fifteen
minute rant and he grew
blacker and angrier by the line
and I was hoping we'd make it
through the evening riot-free.
An elegant woman mispronounced
my name and described me
as the kind of young, promising
poet who would help NYQ move
its future in the right direction

My poem was twenty-five
bare boned lines, without a rhyme
or metaphor in sight, spoken

in plain every day language
about my father. Dinner
was winding down, him
and me were the only ones
left at the table. He changed
chairs, hunched closer to me
and told me they were cutting
back at the factory. He was fifty
years old and if he lost his job
he wouldn't know what to do.

My father would never say
anything like that to anyone
and I just looked at him
until he got up and went
into the living room. I read
in a too low voice that seemed
to be hoping to crack and act
like some kind of man. After,
I thought some girls would talk
to me, tell me how deeply
my poem moved them
as they touched my arm
and said they'd love
to see all of my work,
but their fathers' were not
like mine and no I'd never
be the kind of guy

they'd either take home
for one regrettable night
or to meet their mom.
Instead, I drank a little
more wine, thanked Packard
for including me and took
the subway back to Flushing,
the place where I belonged.

I tried to read my book, but kept
thinking about what it meant
being a poet. Mostly I was glad
no one I hung out with or knew
suspected I could spend hours
in my room writing and cutting
my poems down to size. No one
would call me a faggy artist,
ask me to stand on a car hood
and start rhyming when the night
got long and everyone grew
bored with everything and still
were too scared to head home
to our ever shrinking lives.
But deep down, I felt sure,
if I ever met Moriarty and Baraka
in a late night alley, my poem
would kick both of their poems' asses
with its hands tied behind its back.

John Grey

Outlaw

He wanted to be an outlaw
but no one was hiring.
He graduated from bullying
to shop-lifting to armed robbery
of a gas station
but neither Jesse James
nor Billy Kidd
would move over,
allow him into the pantheon.

He couldn't even be notorious.
The cops raided his apartment,
dragged him down to the station,
but it didn't make the TV news,
was only page seven stuff in the Herald.
Dillinger was too entrenched.
Same with Baby Face Nelson and Clyde Barrow.
He caught no one's imagination.
Not even his own.

He saw a lot of movies
where the bad guy
was the one the audience rooted for.
But the screenwriters stayed away
from his trial, his sentencing,
his five years in the Correctional Institute.
His story just wasn't dark enough
to ever come to light.

John Grochalski

homeless quilt

the cops are smiling
on facebook

beefy knuckleheads
who haven't read a book
except to throw one at you
for some trumped-up bullshit

they are holding up
a group of taped together cardboard signs

a homeless "quilt" they call it in their post

signs they took from people
panhandling on the streets

one sign says

homeless
need help
thank you &
god bless

another says

John Grochalski

trying to make it
anything helps
god bless

there are seven to eight more like it
all bunched together

and the cops in the picture
are smiling their cops smiles
while dressed in their little cop uniforms

they look well-fed
like they've never missed a meal

never not had a roof over their heads
or someone else to wipe their asses

or been stuck on the street
any longer than it takes
to order a cup of coffee

catch their little cop reflection
in a rearview mirror

before marching off to hassle
another broken someone

whom america has gone
and let down again.

John Grochalski

**lone cheer from the
sidewalk for the pissed off
pigeon while casually
forgetting that millions of
people go hungry each day**
—*after Richard Hugo*

he grabs for morsels
he is choking down life

it is raining again
and the weather here
has no clue about the winter

new york city is nothing but a postcard
for television and tourists
this time of year

and i am depressed without end
at the coming of another decade

if i make it
i will see myself become an old man

with old man ideals that have nothing left to burn

John Grochalski

not that this pigeon cares
walking angrily in a circle

tossing lost bagel into the sky
like a cat toying with a trapped mouse

there are more visceral needs
than paying attention to the existential malaise
of another well-fed white man on the street

making comfortable bargains
with father time

like getting bits of food in your mouth
before another pigeon comes along

dodging taxis
and little prick children

or wondering
when this is all over

where your next good meal
is coming from.

John Grochalski

mister lover man of pittsburgh, 1997

i was young
and dumb

thought having my own room
in a run-down cottage
made me a man

and she was golden
and probably sleeping with someone
behind my back

i had lost an old friendship
just to have her
in my bed for a month

and when she smiled
and said
it's over

i stood there
babbling like a fool

at the corner
of murray and forbes

John Grochalski

mister lover man of pittsburgh, 1997

talking sweet nothings
to myself

as she gingerly
walked away.

Michael D. Grover

Confessions Of An american Outlaw #117
(Transmissions For Bob Kaufman)

Who would bite the dead
Something we wouldn't do
What if the dead were to bite back
Like the undead
Like my favorite zombie movie
Or any zombie movie
They all involve the dead biting
Or vampire movies
Maybe biting the living
Would be okay
Under the right circumstances
But I'm a vegetarian
They don't make veggie people
Like they do burgers
& other artificial meat
We'll just have to wait

Stephanie Barbé Hammer

Not an Epitaph

I so don't want to R.I.P.
Let me hang out for a while in
Crunchy tuna roll heaven chat
With the Buddha if he is available
Speak with Moses
St. Joan and
"red" Emma G.
Then let me come back
And kick some karmic ass
Be a doctor or a plumber or
A garbage collector
Or a nurse or a warrior who never
Raises his hand to hurt another
Let me come back and help heal
The seas one plastic bottle at a time
Let me build cabins and teepees
On that reduced 22nd century landmass bring back
The orca and the eagle
Work in a lab to string together the DNA threads
To stitch back the species lost
And stolen by our 21st century greed
Bring me back
I'll roll up my sleeves
I'll do it right
I swear you'll be amazed
By how good
We'll do it
This time.

Stephanie Barbé Hammer

Anti- Pastoral 1 (Coupeville, WA)

1.
Nature you are a pain in the ass the way you rain every time I walk to the mailbox. The silence of the deer in heat is deafening. Then there's the cawing of the birds and the monotony of trees giving oxygen, cleaning the air. "Green is boring," my friend Tim Hatch once told me in an auditorium in San Dimas, and I laughed because IT'S TRUE.

2.
Everyone here sighs "it's paradise" and I respond, "Where's the Macy's?" It's not that I don't like flowers but come on — they're not everything and anyway it's not why we left our little caves looking to invent something that wasn't just wood and water and stone and bone.

2b.
The deer eat all the flowers here anyway.

2c.
Also, there is no recycling here and the garbage is piling up at the dump. NOT cool.

3.
Point of information: Jean Jacques Rousseau was not born in the country and Thoreau had supplies brought in, which Emerson mostly paid for. Jean Jacques wrote about natural man, but he sure beat the hell out of Geneva as soon as he could, and he lived in f****ing Paris and London — probably so he could complain about them.

4.

I complained about the city too when we lived there. So, we moved to the country and now I miss the aggravation: the neighbors screaming, the lights going off, and the helicopters circling at 4 am. Alexander Pope wrote a poem once about a woman looking over her vast country estate. "Odious odious trees," she says.

4b.

I wouldn't go that far but what I wouldn't do for a taco truck and a dry cleaner I could walk to. Even the gurgling splat of someone spitting in the scooter-littered street. The spitter mutters things, and then the bus comes, and you get on behind them, but you hang back just a smidge, in case they resolve to toss another loogie. Your coins sweat slightly in your already smudged palm.

5.

It finally stops raining and the workmen arrive to repair the roof because a pine tree fell on it, right over the bedroom. It could have just driven through like a javelin. We're lucky not to be dead the tree expert tells us. One tree workman is very handsome. He sits in his truck with his blonde hair and eats a sandwich. He tells me he goes fishing on the weekends. I look at my husband sitting at his computer crunching code in his bathrobe, and think I've made the right choice. I mean fishing? Honestly.

Stephanie Barbé Hammer

Pine Cones (Cascades, Washington State)

Me
and
my dad
Walk the
Cascades in the
Woods looking for
Fallen pine cones to
Start the fire with in the cabin—
I don't wear my glasses because
They are new to me and sit strangely
On my ears, so when I pick up the thing
That is brown and mottled like a pine cone it
Just feels wrong. Pine cones are brittle and dry
This brown thing is wet and it's cold so I crouch down
To investigate with my already pretty bad eyes. A slug. I let
Go. Stand up. We walk to the stream skip tiny stones
Never minding about pine cones. But I personally never
Forget the slime-wonder of an aliveness
I thought
Was
Good
Only
To
Be
Burnt.

Brian Harman

Old West

Every once in a blue, I'll take a gander,
watch a Twilight Zone black and white
episode, sometimes set in the Old West,
and maybe it's the same in old Western
movies, but there is a scene, a dialogue
of men with rifles, *what are ya yella*,
they say, and man becomes a lesson,
and before there is a chance to change,
a supernatural of sorts toys with the
audience brains, characters frozen in
frame to show us, what if isolation,
what if destined for, what if fear, what
if man is trapped, what if man is trapped
in a man's world, time being relative
to mind zones, relative to relatives--
the Old West reminds me of my grandpa
Manuel and his John Wayne movies,
a man's love for portrayed manhood,
I wonder, when my grandpa accidentally
stepped on a rusty nail that led to
the amputation of his legs, was he a man
anymore in his own mind, was bedridden
still a man, was being pushed around
on wheels still a man, what becomes
from loss, from being lost, what is carried
on and remembered, what is generations,
what was once, is, can be in the twilight
of the Old West?

Brian Harman

Wild Parrots of Santa Ana

At dusk, an eerie plurality of sound,
squeaks and squawks in lo-fi stereo,
like air raid speakers installed
in the trees near 4th St. and The Frida,
blasting daily audio homages
to Hitchcock's birds, or Dracula's bats,
or the local escape of evilly possessed
Disneyland Tiki Room animatronics,
not at all like sweet Nightingale
melodies or Mockingbird lullabies,
hush little baby, don't, there's no canary
in the window twittering before tawts
of tawing a puddy tat, more like Woody
Woodpecker crazy, Heckel and Jeckel
mischief, an Angry Birds revenge
on thieving Green Pigs, a kind of
parrots for pirates, arduous avians,
the kind, if captured for the home cage,
would bite, claw, chirp until ears bleed,
will tell kids, *Polly wants a fire-cracker*,
the kind of bird like my dad bought
on a whim back in the day, a solitary
lovebird I named Fruit Loop cuz it
was cuckoo, it was lonely, it needed
a mate, to breed, to fly or die and one
day it took flight, the cage "accidently"

Brian Harman

left open, escaped beyond cypresses,
hawks, eagles, falcons be damned,
maybe it survived, maybe vultured,
however long, it was one again with
nature, wild as the Santa Ana winds,
foraging with new flocks on the block,
feasting on exotic plant life, pecking
magnolia blossoms, nut and fruit trees,
beautiful, sticky, vibrant purple,
car-nuisance jacarandas, Pterodactyl
throwback screeches echoing off
buildings, meanwhile fast food seagulls
snatch french fries on beaches while
once revolutionary carrier pigeons
headbob for bread crumbs, those empty
blackhole looking eyes death-staring
shit target humans sipping on nectar
smoothies, tweeting about sadistic
estuaries, existentialism, the closest
thing to touching the evolution of birds--
Superman, airplanes, regurgitation,
suburban nests, feather ruffling, middle
finger posing, using newspapers for things
other than reading, the fear of the call
of the wild lingering; parrots mimicking
reminders of the lost sanctuary.

Curtis Hayes

Good-Time Charley

my dad had a buddy in the navy.
about once a year our phone would ring
and I would pick up
to hear a stranger on the line.
I was allowed to stay up late
most Saturdays
when KTLA Channel 5 ran
B-grade horror movies until 2AM
I'd be up watching things like
The Brain That Wouldn't Die
Day of the Triffids
and Psychomania.
Jimmy lived on the east coast.
he would call late
and when I picked up
he would ask for Zippo Bob,
a nickname I didn't know,
and it was the first time I ever heard a man
slurring his words.
I once asked
why Jimmy only called when he was drunk.
"Things just didn't go the way he wanted,"
my dad would say.
I asked, "Was he a good guy, when you knew him?"
he thought about it.

Curtis Hayes

"He was a good-time Charley.
Good to have around on leave
when the liquor was flowing
and women were around."
I pictured a man in a dark room
staring at a telephone.
my mom had told me
that Jimmy had gone through two wives
and couldn't keep a job.
"He just wants to hear a friendly voice."
and to talk about better times."
I told myself then
that I would never be a good-time Charley,
and some nights
when I'm sitting in a room
with just a TV screen for light
and that urge comes
to pick up my phone and scroll through
the old numbers,

I sometimes wish I'd listened.

Steven Hendrix

untitled (covered in shit)

Live deeply, I told myself
that seems to be the way to live
even if I don't know what it means
don't be another automaton
I learned that from Shelley
and it seems to be in line with
live deeply
but it's hard, a constant struggle
loss of consciousness of the goal
everyday,
a lack of awareness of movement
through life and movement toward
nothing
nothing deep,
only through the piles of shit
that life has dumped on me
movement through the piles of shit
deep beneath
an automaton living deeply
no not deeply, just deep
perhaps living deeply
is the digging out
the searching for flickers of light
that have made it through

finding hope and holding on to it
flickers of hope beneath piles of shit
a flame
a flame to burn through the shit
from within
to rise up
to find a way to climb out of the shit
holding a flame in one hand
and hope in the other
or reaching out with the other
finding another hand
pulling someone out of the shit
with you
maybe this is living deeply
a flame in one hand
a hand in the other hand
covered in shit
but rising above

Steven Hendrix

Metaphors in Search of a Love Poem
—after Donna Hilbert

I
When the petals of the flower wilted
fell to the earth, shriveled
the arms of the sun reached down
blew off the loose soil
placed each one back on the stem

II
The river washes over the rough stone
smoothing the edges, then recedes
allowing the stone's translucent rainbow
to reflect the radiant sunlight

III
The scalding coffee embraces
the frigid ice cube
absorbs its concern
compromises on a mutually
propitious temperature

IV
An uneaten carton
of expired ice cream
remains in the freezer

Steven Hendrix

Air and Understanding

You describe for me the magnitude of your pain,
You tell me, prematurely, of your need for my support,
You expect me to remember when I'm least likely to,
And then, in a dark moment, as exhaustion sets in,
Exhaustion from having two jobs (mine),
Exhaustion from having no job (yours),
Exhaustion from the hunger of nothing to eat and the hunger
    to succeed,
Looking for release, a moment a reprieve,
You find a way to shift your guilt, or self-deprecation, or
    sense of despair onto me,
Through small verbal jabs, and then left hooks, and finally
    upper-cuts,
Until I forget I'm supposed to feel sympathy,
Until I forget I'm supposed to give support,
Until I forget I'm supposed to ease your pain,
And I strike back with a rhetorical knockout,
My words harsher than the dull blade of a fishing knife.
And now finally I feel something in my frozen heart, in my
    numb limbs, in my hyperpractical mind,
I'm finally cognizant on an emotional level,
Now that I see you crumble to the floor,
Crying, hyperventilating, gasping for air and understanding.

Ted Jonathan

The Boy Who Never Came of Age

Summer in the upstate bungalow colony
is going great for this 13-year-old. His
brutal father remains back in the Bronx,
and peer pressure that hamstrung the boy
there eased here. Girls are crazy about him.
He's crazy about girls. Fooling around
in and out of the swimming pool, playing
pinball, Karen and Dory asking to see
his dick, apple picking, his almighty hard
on, being struck by a heady strange notion:
I can be me. But tomorrow is summer's
end. His mind echoing Dory telling him
to meet her at 7 by the jukebox in the lounge
of the Bollinger Hotel. Big brown glistening
eyes, she said she wanted them to *share*
a night to remember. Wanting his chance
to be alone with Dory more than anything,
he's game but jumpy. Same day his father
appears. After supper, Mom feels threatened,
asks her boy not to go. Unlike his father,
he's sickened by violence. But he's no
momma's boy, and swore to himself he'd
grab his Tony Oliva bat and bash the fucker's
head in should he ever hit his mother again.
No thinking. Swing hard, over and over.
Mom persisted, pleading with him not to go.

Ted Jonathan

Eyeing his father, the boy, hot for Dory
and wanting to believe Mom would be safe
amid this cluster of adjoining bungalows,
is gone. A mile into the starlit night ...

At the lounge, The Animals' "Sky Pilot" sets
him right. A sloppy kiss with lots of tongue
turns long and passionate. He forgets
he's nervous. She's lavender. Then there's
shouting, "Ted! Ted!" It's Nat, Karen's kid
brother, hopping around like a spastic
marionette. "Ted! Your mother!" Running
past Nat, into the blackness that minutes ago
shined all luminous and starry, he wants out
of his body, like during emergency hernia
surgery when he was a little etherized boy.
But he's in his body, a horse galloping
steadily, wanting not to get there ... An adult,
he doesn't recall who, pulls him into a bare
room in a bungalow ... left there alone ...
thwack of a slamming door ... No one telling
him his mom is dead. And his father, the killer.

Robert Jay

Four Dog Haiku

Those handsome sad eyes
A dog looks at you again
Already knowing

Back and forth all day
Waves ceaselessly playing fetch
With dogs on the beach

Shitting on the lawn
Even the dog looks ashamed
In such proud suburbs

I envy those dogs
So happy, oblivious
To our tragedy

Robert Jay

Karmic Chrysalis

Mindful footsteps fall
Careful and compassionate
By the monks of the monastery
Between caterpillar crawls
Along walkways leading into
Their next life to be reborn
As bodhisattva butterflies

Robert Jay

Letting It Warm Up

Waking up to car alarms
Wiping my night crusted eyes
Windshield clear transparent
Defrosting my frigid bleak
Nerves to fire on all synapses
Checking the crucial fluid levels
Of coffee always down too low
Getting my own shit in gear
Finding the ignition
Turning it over
Again and again

Luke Kuzmish

Pigeons

I was jealous
of the pigeons huddled
together on the wire
overlooking the projects
covered in snow

jealous of the brotherhood
found in misery
the common enemy
of winter chill and
the biting wind

jealous of the consolidation
all their problems
narrowed to survival alone

jealous of the potential
high on the wire

Luke Kuzmish

Patrick Says

Patrick says
he knew
if he didn't learn to love
other people or himself
—what's the difference?—
he would die a junkie

Patrick says he might
be able to stay clean for
a while:
long minutes where
hope is birthed
and dies between the pulse
of the punch clock

Patrick says he can't love
you or
anyone
if he
needs
your love
because then it's just business
or addiction
—what's the difference?—
but Patrick says
he won't die
under that thumb

Marie C Lecrivain

Lie Detector

in the near future
all journalists will be
equipped with lie detectors
to keep away opinions
disguised as fake news

and spawn job growth
for those who'll learn to interpret
labyrinths of squiggly lines

there'll be more masseuses
and life coaches to keep
reporters on point
confident and comfortable
in the honesty zone

bookmakers will lay odds
on which network anchor
shares bad news best

and Ipsy will release
a new line of sweat-free
skin care products
for their new subscribers

the world will be better
with a truth driven media
we can access 24/7

substitute "politician"
for journalist
and see what happens

Jennifer Lemming

Cloaked

Hoodies pulled up and hearts drawn
in the snow, this is my life,
these fractal glimpses into my soul.

In the morning at work I glance out
of my office window at the empty lot
across the street where I see a heart,
heel-scratched out in the snow
by some would-be admirer of a co-worker,
and I can, for a brief moment,
secretly pretend that heart is for me.

At lunch in the break room I pass
members of the tech department
our maintenance workers on
the information highway. When they lunch
together, I overhear their tech lunch-speak,
and I try not to snigger about their vague
references to in and out latency,
and their talk about how best to use
without offense, a thin or fat client.

After digesting my own threat landscape,
with its drive-by downloads,
I wander back to my office,
waiting for the next data cascade
to hit my desk.

Jennifer Lemming

That night, when my husband goes to bed late
and wakes me while he is standing by the bed
with his hoodie on and lights are low,
he wonders why I scream in fright
at the strange, cloaked man that I see
through my sleepy eyes.

He climbs into bed with his hoodie pulled up
against the cool room-draft, and we snuggle
down deep, and I reach into his hoodie
with my warmed hands around his cold ears
and pull him close so we can kiss ourselves to sleep.

Jennifer Lemming

This Winter

This cold is getting old, a finger-numbing,
sniffle inducing old. This cold.
Agitating the creakiness in my bones.
Old this cold has become, where his cold

even stiffens my eyelid folds, Struggling
to awaken in the chill, this cold hangs
them heavy with sleep where I
snuggle under blanket folds.

This cold oldens my resolve to go out
for a walk, to gaze at the moon at night
in the fresh air instead of framed
 by the window sill, still there is beauty

that syncs with the cold. Taut lungs, filled with cold air,
Yet infinitely expanding in a way
that summer cannot, with distorting,
smothering, heat.

The beckoning cold can lay out
a diamond surface road toward the horizon,
an infinitely different, ageless glass spectrum
With more than any other season
can throw at you.

Cynthia Linville

Valley Fire
(September 2016)

We are the last
to set foot in this house,
the last
to sleep in this bed,
to see these green trees.

After we shut this door
and turn this key,
all evaporates into
ash and stone,
into memory.

Cynthia Linville

The Kindness of Strangers

But I'm lost, she says
then tells a complicated story
about a boat (no, a car)
about a friend
(well, no, an ex-husband)
who stole her purse
her phone
her youth,
who left her shivering
in a sequined halter dress,
limping in a broken shoe.
Now she is trapped
looking like a racoon
wandering Rodeo.

Cynthia Linville

Frozen Solid

Silence is the sound of snowfall.
Something with fingers—
uncompromisingly tragic—
reaches in,
closes a door,
whispers nothing with frosty breath.

* * *

Frosty breath closes a door,
reaches in.
Something whispers *nothing*,
touches snow
with tragic fingers.

* * *

Tragic fingers close *something*,
whisper silence
over frozen doors.
Frosty breath becomes snow.

John Macker

Auroras (a solstice poem)

Friends I know who just lost
their infant son went to Norway to
see the northern lights
to become smaller   more granular
to save themselves from the
center of the universe
to become like winter wind
no conscience   no family ties
no human touch or guilt
the nihilist's caress   until
the words that exit their numb mouths
are bare trees forbidden to
breathe spring.

In another latitude December has yet
to take its relationship with winter public
in another latitude they stay in an igloo
and bask in the hallucinatory colors of
Christmas solar winds make of the midnight sky.
They took each other apart
and reassembled their haggard selves
with new words in the snow.
In another latitude I've aged without
the experience of such loss burying me
in open space or
leaving me to my own ashes.

John Macker

This morning in the cold car
kd lang sang "Hallelujah" and
I held Julian and the sun's first
faint warmth of the day close
to my heart that sometimes hibernates
in bare trees or takes solace in empty skies.

John Macker

Abundance
—*For Stewart Warren*

An 80 year old woman in New Mexico
does tai chi in the dog park
in an abundance of presence
shares the rhythms of her age
gathers in and then releases the
shiftless summer air.
In Iceland activists hold a funeral for a famous
glacier, on the permanent plaque they
placed, in English and Icelandic,
is written to the children:

Only you know if we did it.

In Auden's memorial poem to Yeats
he wrote: *Mad Ireland hurt you into poetry.*
Out the window a police car siren's
pulsating shriek cleaves the morning
into two organic halves, one an act of faith
the other, not so much. We were instructed
by the nuns to say a prayer or cross
ourselves every time we heard one
until the danger became
innocent whispered echo.

John Macker

As if nobody had been hurt.

Ireland will plant 400 million trees in the
next 20 years to combat climate change.
So many more will recognize *El Degüello*
when they hear it than those who've
memorized "The Second Coming".
A poet friend in New Mexico
in his last days of hospice
always traveled his own rivers
now they change course, fill him
with their own abundance, tell him
we have all the time in the world.

The purple morning uplifted cosmos petals
a day after rain and the land which has withstood
the emancipation of all these latest hells

never stops singing.

Tamara Madison

Before the Internet: Reading Porn at 14

I swiped it from the carousel in the back of the store
that held the pulp books, the kind with crooked type
and no pictures on the covers. At 14, I couldn't buy it
but it fit easily into my jacket pocket so I took it home.
My best friend and I read it in the bathroom:
tales of a guy named Zeno with a throbbing, veined
"manhood" and later, an eager red-haired teenager
with a long dong. Somewhere there was a trip
to Mexico and a scene with a woman whose body
was described as a "carcass"; there was a chocolate
eclair that burst and also a five-year-old girl who,
after a time, reacted in a "womanly" way
to the goings-on. We read the book in fits and starts
over several days, each time looking at one another
with horror and flinging it away with sick stomachs.
Nothing in our experience had prepared us for this
and it did nothing to ready us for the mundane sex
of real-life. But somewhere stitched through
these scenes that shocked us so was a humor
which did not escape us, and it was the title
that had caught my eye as it gazed from the wire
shelf: "Poked and Pried Open". I wonder now
about the author, imagine a homely man
with a big imagination and a need to fund his own
writing ambitions. As for me, I became a teacher.

Tamara Madison

To My Neighbor with the Plastic Lawn

Your plastic grass is no match
for the Bermuda grass that woke
from memory's sleep, found purchase
in the lip of soil that edged around
the plastic seam and now climbs over
what is fake and clean, and spills
dry spindles in a swell of dusty green.
Your plastic grass can't smother
all that sleeps inside the soil
but even so your plastic grass
will one day have the last
and loneliest laugh: when all of us
have gone to dust your plastic lawn
will rise in wiry strings up from the sod.
triumphant and immortal as a god.

Tamara Madison

Women in Porno Films

Women in porno films just love everything –
anywhere, any act, any orifice and always
with enthusiastic moaning and absolutely no
foreplay. Women in porno films wear
their enormous globular breasts like gargoyles
on a gothic cathedral and perform amazing stunts
with their mouths on the colossal organs
of the men in porno films. Women in porno films
are like love dolls only real, with pulses,
warm blood, and everything except pubic hair,
and as every film reaches its inevitable climax
involving an act that used to be called perverted,
the women in porno films make it clear that they
are ready for more – any time, any act, any orifice.

Do high school girls who walk the halls
in low-cut tees with butt cracks showing
watch these porno films with their boyfriends,
lips parted, panting, in the blue light
of a smart phone screen, feel that they have to act
like the women in porno films? It all makes me
nostalgic for the 70's feminists, not just
the women with hairy armpits and no makeup
(who needed men as much as fish needed bicycles)
but all the brave trail-blazers who fought
for women's right to have careers, families *and*
orgasms, who shouted, protested and burned
their bras all in the name of equality.

Betsy Mars

Sunnyside Care Home

Privacy curtains drawn, we watch Jeopardy.
Our nightly routine, a bond
before parting. The tray pushed aside—
broth and blended brown mounds,
reeking of spoon-fed infancy.

We listen for questions to which
we know the answers.
In the same room, behind curtain number 2,
a man keeps a vigil, silent like his silent twin,
united again in this sterile womb.

Final Jeopardy after the next commercial break;
we wait expectantly. Before the question can be revealed,
a soft voice from behind the curtain requests our pardon.
We mute the TV; he tells us his brother has just passed.
In solidarity we turn off the TV.

That's how death can happen—
the question we will never know.

Daniel McGinn

Sweeping the Shop Floor

I'm about 4'11", walking behind a push broom with a three-foot base, sweeping curls of hair—brown, black, blonde, gray—clipped and scattered like leaves on the beige floor of my father's six chair shop. In this Los Angeles suburb, it's hot in the summer, my eyes itch and the air smells like it's burning; a cross between asphalt sweat and a smoking pie forgotten in an oven. Barbers talk to each other above my head, but I'm not listening. It's Saturday afternoon, the day I get to see my father. I have a shoeshine stand in front of the shop. It's a boy's clubhouse—no girls allowed—there's always a ballgame on the tiny black and white television and magazines dropped at random angles on the line of chairs— *Esquire, True Detective,* and, of course, *Playboy.*

It's five A.M. as I write this. I bring this up because my father is an old man now, he doesn't lift his feet when he walks, and I hear his slippers shuffling in the hallway. He might turn right into the bathroom, or he could turn left and appear in the living room where I am seated in a recliner, writing. He pokes his head into the doorway to see if I am awake.

He asks, *What are you doing?*
A timed writing exercise, I tell him.

Daniel McGinn

I'd ask for three more minutes but he has dementia and wouldn't understand. I have to be the adult in this and every situation.

Do we have coffee? He always asks.
Yes, but I'll have to make it. I reply,

and the morning begins on his terms. My father lives with us. He was dropped on our doorstep like a sentence, interrupted.

Daniel McGinn

The Funerals

My sister stood onstage
at my mother's memorial and spoke
about how lucky she was to be
in the same bed as my mother
when she died; washing the body
gave my mother a proper send-off
and brought closure to her and my sisters.

She spoke with authority.
I had no idea what to say.
My mother and I rarely spoke
before she died. She followed me
like a ghost for a couple of days
until we forgave each other.

I needed to believe that
to get through the first stage of grief
but I don't believe in ghosts
and I avoid going to memorials or funerals.

My father is going to die in my guest room,
he doesn't know that yet—
or prefers not to think about it—
but that's what he came here to do.

Daniel McGinn

I talked to him about advance funeral plans;
he won't address such plans directly
or acknowledge the possibility
that he could die.

We talk about death in general. He doesn't
believe the spirit stays with the body,
and he doesn't visit resting places.
We have a lot in common.

Cremation would be alright.
He would prefer a wake
to a funeral, with plenty of alcohol
and music, because he's Irish
and that's what the Irish do.

My father sometimes sleeps
for an entire day—or a day and a half
if he's really tired—only waking up
to use the restroom.

He did that once
during the first week he lived with us.
He didn't react when I spoke
and tried to wake him.

Daniel McGinn

I stood at the foot of his bed
for a long time, listening
to hear him breathe, and that's when
I came to understand why he was with us.

The next day, he mentioned it.
He knew I was listening
and he tried to not make breathing noises.

He made a few jokes about me
waiting for him to die
and asked if it was safe
to eat the breakfast I made for him.

My father remains alive by sheer will;
I guess we all do. His will is stronger
than the changes occurring in his body.

He'll stop being our guest
on the day he decides he's had enough.
I don't have any desire to wash his body.
I'll never be prepared
for the death of my father.

Daniel McGinn

Writers Block

Maybe it's a good thing.
Maybe it's time to shut up,

shut up myself and learn to walk backwards.
I wish I could give myself another name,

another voice to wear like a mask.
I grow so tired of being nice

I have to go back to my room
and sit myself down in the dark.

Ever watch a year go by
and wonder where you went?

Joan McNerney

Deception

Traces of lace cover walkways.
Snow so white it almost blinds us.
You came with a spectacular glow.
I became awed by this splendor.

Everyone was so captivated
by your charm, wit, words.
We wondered if the sun rose
and fell under that magic.

Pure white snow turns gray
from exhaust fumes.
Hardening on roadsides, icy
frost plunge cars into ditches.

Deceived by your wicked smile
and simmering blue eyes.
Tricked by razzmatazz. Only mud
and freezing rain lies underneath.

Some thought the fault was mine.
How could this have happened?
There must be something else.
Something I have hidden away.

Caught in claw of memories now,
regretting the trust given to you.
But I will never be betrayed again
even if hell freezes over.

Michael Minassian

Postcard From a Drunken Sailor

I am convinced if I wrote
what I thought on this blank
space, this white sarcophagus,
your hands would bleed,
then your eyes pop out
bouncing on two rusty springs
like some cartoon character,
while real steam escaped
from each of your perfect ears.

That's me in the photo on reverse
riding on the back of a mermaid
as she teaches me her song,
the sound you are hearing
for the last time.

Michael Minassian

Driving Nightmare

I typed the word hell
into my GPS

it took me straight
to your house—

avoid highway, tolls
and ferries

avoid figments
of your imagination

travel by dragon
or dragonfly

press now to accept
an alternate route.

Robert A. Morris

Corn Maze

I woke up early and walked out into the tall corn,
looked a rabbit in the eye, and it was gone. I moved

deeper into the warm shadows, stalks shushing me
in the near dark. The mocking crow cast curses from

the east as a sun drew the salt from my brow.
I changed rows and directions, retraced footprints over

and over. Trying to find the spot where I began, I broke
out in vertigo, prayed for fire, and walked calmly.

Each step was a mile; each mile a year.

As the sky darkened, I found a new clearing. Stepping
out in terror, my shirt damp and dirty. The wind pulled

the cloth away from my skin, and again, I stood with
cold fever. I saw the rabbit from my youth, looked him

in the eye as he lay lifeless in the clover. My shadow
appeared as an anonymous giant, expanding with my

relation to the pacifist sun. I walked before him, returning
to the tall corn. Each breath was a mile; each step a year.

I walked further still, and the shadow weaved the stalks
behind me, so no one would know I was gone.

Robbi Nester

Allegory

Every year, the storks return
to the same rooftops, flying
toward home in a flurry
of white wings. Loyal to one
place, one mate, this bird
seeks the warmth of winter
chimneys for its nest,
a mess of sticks reordered
every year. An emblem
of good luck, of family,
the stork assures us that
though we humans mar
the world, life will continue.

Sometimes, this persistence
has a price. In a photograph
taken in the wake of World War One,
the storks stand erect as undertakers.
Their wings enshroud gaunt bodies.
Beneath them the skeleton of a house,
reduced to an outline, a child's
black crayon scrawl. This image
reminds us in stark black and white
that some storks are scavengers.
What better hunting ground
than this? Where life persists,
death must also make its home.

Robbi Nester

The Smallest Whale

He's a blue whale, but not as we
have ever seen in life. At birth,
a blue whale spans 26 feet,
can weigh almost 9000 pounds.
Adults can reach 100 feet,
their hearts as heavy as a Buick.

The loudest beasts on earth,
they ring the oceans with their
raucous vocalizations. I know
all this without ever seeing one.
Or actually, I've seen them,
but what I've really seen is just
a fluke, a tail, an eye. Did I
mention that a blue whale's
eye measures 6 inches, probably
their smallest part? It's like
looking at an ancient redwood.
At best, we see the trunk.
The top's so far above us.

Robbi Nester

This whale's alone, in an ocean
bland as a bathtub. No wonder
he looks lost—no pod to guide him,
no swells. Just some ink-blot
jellyfish riding an invisible current.
no color but a misbegotten blue.
By definition, whales are big,
but this one isn't. Does that make him
something else, a whale as we might
make one if we could, innocuous,
almost cute—not the living
contradiction that he is in life,
the biggest creature, eating the smallest
by the ton, our peaceful neighbor?

Martina Reisz Newbery

Sadie and the Sea

Sadie tells me she has had sex
with the ocean. She says
that it began with a wave
which came up behind her
and a door in that wave
swung open.

At first, she says,
she was afraid, but went anyway,
deep into the doorway
into a room of blue-green wet
and salt and whispers
from a bed of sand.

She was stroked
and lightly sanded and the water
enveloped and entered her
with a tenderness reserved
for its frailest creatures.
She was, after that, she tells me,

a "nympho on the half shell,"
shameless in the face of foam and tides.
Sex with the ocean, said Sadie,
is similar to sex with angels
(which I have had
on numerous occasions),

although to be perfectly honest,
angels are heavier than the ocean —
more cumbersome,
more insistent,
more intrusive; not as slick,
not as salty.

In the past, I've found
Sadie's stories difficult to hear.
She tortures her days with Truth —
the straight stuff —
and I prefer my reality peppered
with, at least, a few fictional embellishments.

That being said,
my late-night dreams
explode with this particular
tale's implications. What to say
except, "Good night, Sadie.
Good night."

Martina Reisz Newbery

Phases of the Moon

There is no man or woman
in the moon,
but we become the moon
and end up appraising ourselves,
all reflections of ourselves,
in lakes and ponds and
on the surface of well water.

When we walk on the grass
on a June morning,
say in Vermont or Maine
or North Carolina
and the drops of the
previous night's rain
lay large as an owl's eyes

on the green blades,
we see ourselves and,
what we see there
(or anywhere for that matter)
wants more than anything
to be whole, fully understood,
fully desired.

Natalie Peterkin

Shame

on long drives i would
settle into the soft, black interior
of my dad's Nissan Altima
it was always freshly vacuumed
and had the scent of his cologne
he would play Motown hits
or jazz
but the smooth jazz
that all sounds like different versions of
The Girl From Ipanema
i would sit and drift softly
through my own thoughts
parsing through obsessions
endlessly reimagining
things that had happened
should happen
might happen
probably won't happen
but could happen
the highway flew past
asphalt and commuters
i pretended to look
i knew
somehow
this much thinking
was wrong

Natalie Peterkin

The Meaning of Life is in A Pile on the Floor

I sneeze and
everything that has ever meant anything
gets all over the carpet.
My roommate is using the broom and dustpan
For what, I am not sure.
We do not talk much.

Outside, a single stream of rain pounds on the window.

I look and
everything that has ever meant anything
looks a lot like dust.

Rob Plath

trigger unhappy

if i'm not punching the fuck out
of the keys of the poetry machine

if i'm not drunkenly conducting
w/ paint brushes over the canvas

if i'm not madly brailling
the fretboard in the dark

then the violets in my holsters
turn back into revolvers

& i draw on myself
& blow away my peace

Rob Plath

thru busted blinds

i left the lights on
& before i slip the key in
the front door lock
i get the urge to peer
into my own place
thru the window
w/ busted blinds
there are no people
waiting for me
just an old green couch
& a broken down rocker
a boarded up fireplace
a carpet full of cigarette burns
two lopsided stand up lamps
suddenly from this perspective
i'm not so sure i want
to enter anymore
perhaps even tho it's cold
i'd be better off
outside beneath the stars
but then i spy the desk
the black typewriter
peeking out enough
to see a tier of keys

& then suddenly the cat
leaps up on a high shelf
& sits on the corner
diamond yellow eyes glowing
like the soul of the room
& i leave the stars
& unlock the door

Rob Plath

just a man & a guitar

elliott smith reluctantly
performed his song
"miss misery"
at the 1998 Oscars

sandwiched between
michael bolton's
"go the distance"
& céline dion's
"my heart will go on"

he never recovered...

(RIP dear elliott)

Jeanette Powers

How We Move On
—for Jeremiah Walton

Baby Bear is a dirty kid who uses my backyard firepit
to burn his journals in a Ceremony of Passage

we haven't invented new mythologies for centuries
and they become my first Vestal Virgin, a living altar

to the Nows of Travel and Homecoming and How
To Let Things Go That Once Were a Story Made of Iron.

How do we change the way we worship and murder?
Who can bid me arise from the Mist without chains?

There's an empty leash on the porch tied to a hand-woven
rope
that used to keep my dog from running off into the wild.

Their pages float, charring up into the wind and are caught
on thermals, youth glows then turns to ash.

I watch from the kitchen window, still covered in frost
along the edges, I grow colder with distance.

I try not to think of my inner child dying with that dog
I invent that his death doesn't kill my longing to play and be
loyal.

Baby Bear adds another book to the fire, it falls open
and the edges of the paper burn to the center.

Jeanette Powers

Dogmeat (the fish)
—for Isaiah Devine

I recognize this boy
ten, maybe eleven years old
in the pool hall begging games off the men
who will all teach him a thing or two
about cues, shots and scratches.

This is the same long hair and tight shoes boy
I met at the town fair on a Friday night
where I was working the ticket booth
with the bank ladies and retired vets
and this boy comes up to me all smiles
with cotton candy in one hand
and a tiny white and orange goldfish in the other
won from one of the ring toss fair games.

This fish is dogmeat for sure
it'll never survive the tilt-o-whirl, the ferris wheel
I mean it's got like two hours of air in that plastic sleeve
he pushes the fish into my line of sight
he's got me pegged as the bleeding heart all right
and says: *Hey, do you want this fish?*

Jeanette Powers

Every part of my being says *absolutely not*
except for my mouth, which blurts out sure
because this boy and me and that fish
have one thing in common
we all know what it's like to not have a shot.

The kid runs off with his friend to the next ride
and I get off my shift and drive to the 24-hour superstore
and get a tank and food and a bubbler and water ph toner
laughing with Nathanael about how much it takes
to keep a measly goldfish alive
and my friend names him "Dogmeat"
because we're still not sure he'll survive.
Now, months later
drinking whiskey at Padgett's Pool Hall
in this small town nowhere Missouri
this kid comes right up to me
asks: *how's the fish doing?*

Fine. Growing big and strong.
I say, and it's true.

The kid runs back to the pool table
he's biting his tongue and holding up
the too-heavy cue stick, one eye on the ball.

We're both counting on him making it.

Oops

I threw open the drapes,
groggy from a sixteen hour shift.
It was 1:00 o'clock
on a scorching Sunday.

Outside two kids from the building
were throwing a ball.
Their little sister was playing
with her Star Wars action figures.

I smiled and waved at the three of them,
taking a sip from the warm beer on my nightstand.

The two boys
stopped their ball game,
staring at me.
The little girl looked up and laughed,
pointing at me.
I watched her run down the sidewalk,
shouting something in Spanish.
Her mother came out of their apartment,
scooped the child into her arms.

Wendy Rainey

It took a few moments
for me to realize
that I was stark naked.

I looked at the boys
who were still staring,
motionless.
One of them looked frightened.
The other had his mouth open.
I spotted their mother,
fists clenched,
marching up the path
in my direction.

I yanked the curtains closed,
popped open a fresh beer,
and fell back into bed.
Wondering if the damage
was permanent.

Wendy Rainey

Primal Urges

Snout shoved in my crotch.
Radar dish ears.
Warm breath on my lips.
She's more woman
than I bargained for.

I'm scanning dog obedience
on my phone
while she drags me down the block.
Sunglasses flying,
I stumble over her,
kissing the hot gravel road.

Back at the house
I make a ham and swiss on rye
and phone the veterinarian.
I say, "Spay,"
they say, "Hold, please."
Her big brown eyes
study every move I make.
When I reach for the sandwich on the counter
she leaps in the air,
grabbing it in her mouth,
knocking the phone out of my hand
with her paw.

Wendy Rainey

I'm still yelling at her,
but she's moved on.
Patrolling the perimeter,
calculating the risk,
planning her escape.
Spotting a handsome Doberman
on a leash,
she scales the fence,
growling,
her body slinking
towards him.

Finally,
I'm with someone
I understand.

Tanya Rakh

your blood

I want to live inside your blood
the layer that coagulates and
dries at daybreak
blends into soil under
root and animal dream

all the insects will know me then
the rot inside my open mouth
will seep into their newborn creatures

you'll know me by the time we awaken
the forest is my vertigo,
spiral tongues alive and waiting
time trickles into slumber
into meals and cyclical
amusements
into cloud cover and rhythm

the white noise of a quiet life
muffled amputations near the fires
there is no other place to rest
no quick evolution for
an aching skeleton

Tanya Rakh

only this
and us
and miles
all time and noise and bleeding seasons
the insects pollinate their homes
feed on this sweetness of
ripe petals
clinging to an empty core, they
shiver under autumn's
leaden sun

Vivid and Livid and Just Plain Scared

He doesn't know the name
of the fucking lunatic
who wanted to paint this dream,
after slamming down health club burrito of cough syrup,
Xanax Hot Pockets,
and grapes soaked in a reasonable tequila,
but he's pretty sure the situation as it's screaming along
called for someone who might be dead.

Or they may have just drawn
too many Batman stories in the 1970s. The ones
where the madness and the weather seemed to be
going about ripping off of the cape and cowl
in a fashion that can gently be described as backwards.

This dream is fucking awful.
The couch is on a highway where you can hear
men and women screaming themselves out of town
and on to the one hundred and seventy-fifth dimension.

And what if traffic picks up?

Gabriel Ricard

This dream is all giraffes smoking cigars,
Woodwards going to the mattresses with the wax museum,
and the razzle-dazzle of entertainment venues
that are obscene and essential in his memories and ambitions.

He would love to wake up now.
He would love to see the artist find work
making someone else sweat hideously
in a situation that is at least supposed to be physically
    liberating.

Or at least just comfortable.
Or dull.

He wakes up,
but then doesn't.

Brian Rihlmann

All Insane

I've heard people complain about it—
"Jeez! Everything's a mental disorder these days!"
and boy, it's true—
you ever pick up
the latest edition of the DSM?

but so what?
I think neurosis
SHOULD be—
MUST be the norm

because if you're happily adjusted
to this artificial existence
this madness we call a life…

this plastic consumer hell
of overabundance, overstimulation
and distraction…

this absurdly perfectionistic
celebrity worshipping nightmare
of a culture…

this shitstorm of lies
pretzeled values
and propaganda…

Brian Rihlmann

if you've made a virtue of servitude—
the vacationless years of thankless jobs
and mandatory overtime…

if you call all this
PLUS drowning in debt
"The Good Life?"

you ain't one of my tribe, brother—
I only understand the ones
who've bloodied their gums
gnawing at the bars of their cages

the ones who'd chew off
their own foot
to get out of this trap

Jason Ryberg

The Kind of Weed

that gets you to thinking that even though you've been
drinking beer, off and on, since about noon (but hell, beer
ain't really drinking, is it, now?) and even though it's been
about 97+ degrees most of the day, and you've been out in it
laboring away with your buddy, swabbing his house
some godawful shade of atomic pea soup vomit green,
still, a couple hits of this stuff after you've called it quits
for the day, has you, suddenly, reinvigorated and fairly
confident that you can make it through all of *the Lord of
the Rings* or *Matrix* trilogy tonight, maybe order some
pizzas and invite some folks over *(YEAH MAN, LET'S
FREAKIN' DO THIS THING!)*, but the next thing you
know is you've woken from what seems like multiple
lifetimes' worth of the weirdest dreams you've ever dreamed:
dreams as real and crystal freaking clear as your Hi-Def
TV screen, here, dreams as freaky as any movie you've ever
seen, dreams just a little too Freudian and Jungian to go into
too much detail, here, concerning, and it must be almost
dawn and you're sitting upright in the middle of the couch,
clothes and shoes still on, a nearly full beer in your hand,
tilted, slightly (at whatever windmill that has most recently
appeared on the horizon of your mind) but still somehow
un-spilled, a movie paused on the TV, and somewhere, birds
starting to sing. Yeah, that kind of weed.

Alex Z. Salinas

Road rage prayer

I need emergency Dial
Soap, Lord, my mouth
Speaks the darndest
Lines during rush hour,
Easy hate spreading like
Wolf spider poison in vein
Canals and I wonder,
Where else has it bore
Holes in my heart?
Halting at stoplights
Cursing one's dark
Skin, beautiful
Singing, old age,
Aimless female gaze.
I must kill it, The Beast,
Right here right now.
Lord, rescue me from
Disease passed for tradition.
Give me the strength to
Honk my horn
If I have to, if I must.

The Death of Cash

Oh, great arbiter, dealmaker!
Oh, great universal equalizer and exchange!
Your days are as numbered as the very dates
and denominations on your various faces.
Too slow, too risky, too tangible.
We will not slice our fingers,
fill our coffee cups, cup holders or piggybanks.
No mattress will swell with you.
No clay pot will entomb you, safe from thieves.

We do not count any more.
We simply swipe and log in, more handy
than some furtive fumbling
in a wallet or purse.
We have left you in a safe somewhere in Switzerland
backed by no gold or legal tender.
So removed we are from bartering two chickens
for a bushel of wheat,
from precious metals being precious.

Oh clinker, oh crinkler!
Oh colorful paper, greeting card enhancer,
suitcase stuffer with bands and belts,
coin of the realm, coin of the slot machine,
cheap payment for someone's thoughts!

Jeff Santosuosso

Oh cash, will we find you on a cave wall,
a scroll, or a great stone in the Middle East?
You built a world
and bore your epithet as the root of all evil
with Lincoln's stoicism engraved on your copper.

You grimy, disease-ridden, filthy lucre!
There can be no well-wishes without you.

Linda Singer

Dysphoria

To stand still, in the middle
of a Ralph's parking lot,
on a rainy day, unable to decide
where to go, how to feel

with an empty shopping cart
under dark clouds
allow myself to simply
linger.

Feel the confusion.
It's tolerable. Nothing
is going to happen
if I simply stand,
muddled, staring,
between parked cars,

like one of these
thirsty trees,
on this asphalt,
next to the
cart return,
waiting.

Linda Singer

At the Table

Give me your tired, your poor,
your yearning to breathe free,
I will cover them in thermal
blankets and bed them down

where they will sleep soundly
on soft, comfortable, concrete floors,
where nightmares will chase them,
where they will find no peace.

Send me the wretched waste,
of your teeming shore.
I will separate mother,
child, father, husband, wife.

I will shove them, unwashed,
into squalid, crowded cells,
beneath chain link shadows,
below an imposing steel-slatted wall.

There, in my care, children,
alone, separated, parentless,
caged and confused,
will cry out for empathy.

Linda Singer

There, in my care, children,
of two and three,
will defend themselves
in an immigrants' courtroom.

Then I will turn and ask myself,
who with an ounce of morality
can rest their head
on America's pillow tonight?

Jedediah Smith

Near Enough the Loft

A pigeon lights on the sill of the fourth
story classroom over Valencia Street
where I'm working and we gape at each other
through the window in equal surprise. Its
vermilion eye seems the opposite of natural
and naked pink feet squirm wormily
gripping the ledge and I feel faint
revulsion for this flapping disease.
Do the mad city crowds breed such contempt?
Maybe it's our words, those puffs of air
that clip our thoughts, which have failed us:
when we say pigeon, we mean filthy—
when we say dove, we mean holy—
when we say squab, we mean tasty—
but all are genus Columba, the same bird
and a word that means swimmer of the air.
When we first domesticated them ten
thousand years ago, we must have seen
something of ourselves in them that we could
look at and call comrade. The male bows to
his lady in courtship, mates for life,
and helps feed their young. A symbol of love
from the offer of olive leaves to Noah
to the flocks weaving around Audrey
Hepburn and Gregory Peck on the Spanish
Steps in *Roman Holiday*. Gluttons, they

Jedediah Smith

prefer churros dropped by vendedores to
birdseed. Cowardly, they fly from danger,
but no matter how far, they always return
home. Looking in the face outside my
window is like looking in a mirror: so
similar but still reversed. Like us they crowd
city sidewalks glowering, but we sink only
lower over time past concrete and asphalt
to dark earth which drops away from the
pigeon who is pulled up by the sky from
the shadows of buildings into full sunlight
until the feathers are too white to see. From
the highest stories, a city is wind, streets
below nothing but a distant babble running
over stone. Up here, people become rare
enough that human and bird can meet as
comrades again. From my room, I can see
secret coops above flat-topped Victorian
rowhouses, hard men with yardbird tattoos
and razor scars defy San Francisco
ordinances to become rooftop Assisi's
preaching to the birds. They cup pigeons
gently and coo and kiss the backs of their heads
before launching them into space where they
circle for a time until called back down,
willing to relinquish the air in return
for the joy of welcoming hands.

Jedediah Smith

Morning Is a Nationality

We teem together on the 7:02 Daly City train
        commute, yearning
for paychecks and more coffee.
At each stop lines shuffle forward
still tired, huddled, massing
around stanchions
tripping over briefcases and toolbuckets.

Rain-sogged herringbone releases steam,
and breath fogs windows
until the air is dopey and hot.
Cars rock, tempest-tost
while late risers strive to draw straight eyeliner
        and gloss lips
as tracks tunnel
the harbor that twin cities frame.

24th Street Mission stop at 7:54
up the escalator to open air
and clouds rain-black
and everything suddenly honks.

Step into China Express & Donuts shop
for crullers and coffee to charge up.
The menu offers

Jedediah Smith

Chow Mein con Camaron
Sopa de Wonton
Spagetti con Pollo

A Grindmaster 4 Gallon Automatic Coffee Brewer with 6
Warmers
bubbles behind the counter
with 4 more Bunn warming rings
up front for self-service.

Sign over the rice cooker reads

WE RESERVE
THE RIGHT
...
SERVICE
TO ANYONE

the middle lines faded away by steam.

Every accent from Somalia to Beijing orders their donuts
        chock-lut,
chock-lut, men lean over orange trays heaped
with rice or dunk sinkers in mugs.

Jedediah Smith

A young woman nods at the corner table
in an after-meth crash, the owner sweeps
around her and mildly commands the familiar litany:
"Wake up, you gotta go, you need ambulance? Not a motel."

His purple-haired wife behind the counter
skypes on a tablet with their kids back home,
coaxes them to dress faster, eat faster,
gathers and wings them off to school.

Outside again, the clouds have passed
        but awnings still rain fat drops
and the *San Francisco Chronicle* vending box
opens a window to Russian airstrikes in Syria.

Up the ramp to the Mission Center,
elbow the handicapped button
and the gold-framed doors slowly open.
Unlock the classroom at 8:20,
and students begin to migrate in:
        Eboni, Omar, Persia, Lamberto.
Class starts at 8:40
                when we open books together
to negotiate phrases, clauses, and conjunctions
into one common language.

Jedediah Smith

Cross Town Balmy Alley Traffic

   It's Sunday morning, so we go
to the Free Farm Stand in the Mission
for chard, kale, and crunchy old
bread. First, onto BART from
Concord under the bay and layers
of selenium rich silt and metallic
schools of mercury quick smelt. Out
to urine airy heat of 24th street stop
beside labor's redbrick at 2786-4
then down tabasco sidewalks along plaster
walls and red-tile roofs and 3 story walkup
Victorian wood hung with green, white,
and red eagle streamers, gold curves of
Dorados Sinaloense pennants, bright
honeycomb tissue balls. Past silent
Zipcar lot and the Napper Tandy pub
mixing sour Guinness breeze with pastrami
cross street from Mixcoatl Arts and Crafts
and Chilli Cha Cha taunting us with
spicy coconut milk soup topped by lemongrass
and kaffir lime leaves, we round the
corner after Adobe Books and Arts Coop
and up Folsom a block to Parque Niños
Unidos to the Farm Stand.

Jedediah Smith

                    We meet Lisa
smiling, jumping in sneakers, camera eyes
composing shots. "Take a number please"
for harvest giveaway, an hour to go, so we
head back to 24ᵗʰ and Philz for coffee and dogs
guard the door demanding belly scratches
for passage. I get big cup of Jacob's Wonderbar
blend from Garfunkel behind counter
says, "so far so GREAT!" Jenni gets Mint
Mojito iced, wet leaf scent reminds me of
sunless dew on yerba buena around
Milagra Ridge trails. We three prance
to Alley Cat Bookstore for a copy of April
issue of *Curve* with "Size Queens" article
and photo shoot featuring Lisa and girlfriend
in latest erotic chic while Maria Kochetkova
contorts on cover of *Dance* bringing *Giselle*
to SF again this year while her old Bolshoi
lover Sergei Filin visiting US this month
brings *Giselle* to NY so both will battle
ghost queen Myrta and the dance of death.
                              Back
at the stand we wait for our ticket
to be called and receive our day-old bread,
mustard greens, artichokes, and
loquats from Alemany Farm, Persian
Limes from a friend in Santa Barbara,

Jedediah Smith

lettuce and stinging nettles from
backyard garden, lemons from
neighbor Janet. And summer starts:
tomato, pumpkin, and squash seedlings.
        Goodbye to Lisa
back to *Obedient Daughter* film-work
while Jenni and I wind our way back
through murals of morning glory vining
from a violin held by the pupil hand
and among prickly nopal watched over
by Don Hidalgo and La Llorona. An
extraterrestrial head at Capp St. looks
beyond a frame of saguaro red and
yellow, shouts NO ONE IS ILLEGAL
and Laura Campos is right! We are
all aliens, barely belonging,
looking for lovers, brief visitors to
this mostly metal earth. There is
a mural behind the mural, Campos above
Las Mujeres Patricia Rodriquez and
Graciela Carillo above Orozco and
Rivera. We descend through sedimentary
strata to the tunnels and trains and
home.

Joan Jobe Smith

Auto Body Man's Daughter

Princesses Elizabeth and Margaret of England
perhaps rode in shiny automobiles as nice as
my father's 1938 Al Capone LaSalle with a
back seat big enough for two of me if I'd been
twins to toss and turn in all the way to Texas
or his vanilla ice cream-colored '39 coupe with
velvet opalescent upholstery soft as butterfly
wings and rumble seat a count and countess
might've used for champagne soiree while
Caruso in person sang Ave Maria, his spats
propped upon the running board. At age 12
when I wore a baseball cap and thought I was
a boy I asked my father to take me to work with
him to show me how to sand, mask and paint new
Fords, Studebakers, Packards, how to hammer dents
from Cadillac and Chevrolet fenders. Had my father
been a mathematician, I'd've longed to know
parabola, had he been Galileo, I'd've gazed at
sun-beamed aurora borealis but he said NO, you're
a girl, you should do girl things so I did, drearily,
but today, an auto body man's daughter, I wear a
T-shirt I had made with a blow up of his 1955
business card, Ray's Paint & Body Service my
T-shirt says and if my father were still alive he'd
probably smile, perhaps glad I honor him, my
Michelangelo father who could smoke a Lucky
Strike cigarette in one hand, hold air compressor
gun in the other as he turned dusty rusty metal
into cloisonné and car paint into rivers of stars.

Joan Jobe Smith

Heartthrobs

My Aunt Louis subscribed to *Photoplay*
wrote fan letters and kept a movie star
scrapbook for so long that she began to
hallucinate. Boldface lie, my father said,
but I believed my Aunt Louise's story that
the movie star Richard Egan had fallen
head-over-heels in love with her, drove
all the way from Hollywood to Colton,
California, to meet her Saturday afternoons
at the chili dog stand on Mt. Vernon Boulevard.
Just to hold her hand, nothing else,
my Aunt Louise, only 16, swore to her daddy,
a hot-headed Texas railroad man, who got out
his pistol and cleaned it and loaded it and
tried to sneak up on Richard Egan at the
chili dog stand to catch him in the act
with his little girl. But my grandpa always
got there too late, Richard Egan just
having driven away just moments before
back to L.A. in his red '54 Coupe de Ville.
Someday, someday, my grandpa would say,
I'm gonna get me that slippery son of a bitch
and my father would say, Jesus Christ, if this
don't beat all and go outside to grind his teeth.

Joan Jobe Smith

Later, on our way back home to Long Beach
my father'd say if Louise were his daughter,
teen-ager or not, he'd get out his belt and
wallop some sense into her butt and I
knew that he would so I never told him when
Robert Wagner began peeking into my
bedroom window on nights the moon was full.

Joan Jobe Smith

On the Way to Disneyland

It'll be an easy gig, baby, said Richard, my freelance go-go
dance agent, popping my eardrums with the Juicy Fruit
chewing gum he smacked into the telephone receiver,
nuthin' like Whisky a Go-Go, he promised, where the go-go
girl who was to follow me didn't show up and Richard talked
me into dancing her gig, too, four hours straight to The Doors'
"Light My Fie-yarrr"—my poor blistered feet bled for days.
But I hated dance contests, I told him, especially phony ones,
sitting in a stinky smoky bar half the night, pretending to be
an ordinary everyday woman, a housewife or secretary wearing
my tarantula false eyelashes and 3-foot-long false hair, waiting
for the phony dance contest to begin and I'd pretend to want
to be in it, jump onto the stage and undress to my red sequined
bikini and do the Jerk, the Pony, Mashed Potato, the Boogaloo
trying to act like a square, dance geeky to hide the fact I'd been
a professional dancer for months, working for Richard's Rich Street
Agency who also booked the newbie-in-town Goldie Hawn who'd
get discovered that summer and be on tv and make movies.
I also hated acting like I loved to strip like that, always surprised
by the men who drank too much and believed that all women
loved to strip like that in front of a bunch of drunken men,
every time I did it hating myself, losing respect for myself for
perpetuating the myth but the $100 for 10 minutes of dancing
would be the most money I'd ever make in in my life

and the Shimmy Shack Tuesday Night Dance Contest that night
turned out even worse than I expected, Richard booking
Little Egypt who danced in real leopard skins with a real
boa constrictor slithering around her neck as she'd pretended
to be an airline stewardess—and Suzi Q'd been booked, too,
wearing her silver lame 5-inch high heels to match her G-string,

150

Joan Jobe Smith

Suzi Q now a stripper at the Pussycat a Go-Go off Sunset, Suzi
pretending to be a former nun, the drunk guys loving it, believing
it while Little Egypt and then Suzi Q wiggled and writhed to the guys'
thunderous applause and oooh's and ahhh's until too soon it was my
turn to compete in this phony contest and groaned alone in the corner
knowing I had miles to go-go when suddenly a woman from out of the
male maelstrom yelled, "Me! Me! ME next!" and up onto the stage
jumped the most UNordinary 300-pound woman I'd ever seen wearing a
big red-hibiscus-flowered muu-muu and red-tasseled slipper sox. Named
Mary she told Nick the MC and Shimmy Shack owner, dismayed as
Hell, glowering over at Richard sitting at the bar who shrugged and
mouthed, "She ain't one of my chicks" as Mary told Nick she was
a kindergarten teacher from Oregon on summer vacation in Hollywood,
Cally-for-NY-YAY! and she loved to dance! to "Wooly Booly"! So the band
began to play as Mary yanked off her muu-muu but kept on her slipper
sox and ka-pow: all she wore upon her pink, freckled skin were a purple
G-string and purple tassels on two of the biggest most beautiful breasts
I'd ever seen even in the raunchiest men's magazines and Mary could
make one tasseled breast spin one way and the other the other way
big purple propellers they were on the fuselage of pink, twin Spruce
Gooses and the drunken guys at least 200 hundred of them stomp
their feet so hard to the beat of Mary's rock and rolling wooly-
boolying shimmy-shaking that the concrete floor and cinder block
walls of the Shimmy Shack vibrated from this man-made earthquake
and the men hooted and rooted and whistled so loud that Mary won,
hands down, beyond a shadow of a doubt the Shimmy Shack Tuesday
Night Dance Contest—Mary the very first Real Winner of the phony contest
that Nick and Richard had concocted that actually had to pay a Real $500
Prize to a real, ordinary everyday woman, and afterwards Nick and
Richard had a big fight in Nick's office, Nick calling Richard an extortionist

and swore never to hire ever again any more of Richard's go-go girls but
Nick was nice to me, paid me the $100 anyway for not doing anything
and the next day I took my 3 kids to Disneyland
and bought them
Everything they wanted.

William Taylor Jr.

Dearest Friends:

I'm lost again
scrambling for butts
of grace
in the gutters of the afternoon
hiding from anything
that's ever known my name
I'm at the Lush Lounge
where there's beer
and the Kinks playing
on the internet
jukebox thing
so the world holds
together
for a few minutes more
and now it's Blondie
so let's just sit
and drink holding hands
while Heart of Glass
plays forever
and dismiss the darker things
roaming the dirty streets
with our dirty names
in their dirty pockets

William Taylor Jr.

and I tell you
poets today they got
t-shirts and podcasts
they got twitter communities
and micro-blogs
but hardly any poems
worth mentioning
so I don't know
where to turn
but now they're playing
something from
Devo's first record
and that should
get me through
the next line
or two and
after that I
couldn't say.

Kareem Tayyar

The Book of Wandering

The sanctity of not knowing where to start.

Of hearing distant music,
& wanting to know where it's coming from.

Of believing that the myths are all true,
& that there is a river somewhere to be crossed.

Of knowing that there will always be another river.

Of dreaming in languages you don't know how to speak.

Of undressing before a mirror unsure of who you are looking at,
& of falling in love with him anyway.

Of falling forwards,
your eyes closed,
your arms stretched out,
into what you hope will be clouds,
or water.

Of knocking on strange doors,
certain you will be allowed inside.

Of answering to many names.

Of sleeping beneath starlight unsure of where
you will awaken the following morning.

Of the souls of your feet,
which haven't failed you yet.

Kareem Tayyar

It's New Year's Eve

& I'm reading a book
by a 14th Century Buddhist monk whom,
upon turning 40,
built a small hut on the summit
of Xiamu Mountain in China
& spent the rest of his life
as a spiritualist, hermit, & poet.

& here I was impressed with the fact
that I didn't go to a party tonight.

Kareem Tayyar

Los Angeles Diary

Beck is playing on the Highway 101 stereo
traffic-gazing bourbon dreaming vagrants
popping trash-can lids while nightbirds learn
to sing each other's songs

you are Mayor of the Traffic Light
you are the King of Carl's Jr.

& all around you the starlight
seeks its level

& the girl in your passenger seat
asks you what you think of Halley's Comet

chain-link poems with combination locks
are written on the alley-walls of local branches

Wells Fargo cowboy in a leather vest
& matching boots lights a cigarette
first smoked by Gary Cooper

& every sequel is a time-machine

& the Angels Flight funicular
has floated into outer space

Kareem Tayyar

I have exactly four dollars in my pocket
but it's enough to buy a paperback
from the secret bookstore
underneath the lobby of Union Station

I'm just kidding
that place closed down years ago

& don't you know?
the city isn't sliding into the sea

the sea is just returning

Jeri Thompson

I Will Never Forget

Not a day passes I don't think of you.
I hope you're still standing
against the wave you don't see coming.

It's been over a year since we met
at the Psychiatric Hospital,
when you shared your dreams with me;
a class clown, wanting to become a comedian.
And I can't forget your green eyes.

My brother had green eyes too,
before they were scattered by a skeet shot
at point blank range in a vacant field, in 1982.
He didn't have much of a chance either
in his Bipolar world.

I hope you are not returned
to your family in a box,
or homeless again
begging change for the next needle.
I hope your legs got stronger.

You brought my brother back to me.
I learned grieving never ends
but is like the tide that ebbs and flows.

Jeri Thompson

Every Broken Girl

Every broken girl
is looking for her daddy

May hell's darkest shades
shadow the father
who taught his little girl
the way to his heart
is through
his pants.

Jeri Thompson

My Father

The door slams. He is home.
My mother scurries to
Get his dinner on the table
After eight hours at her own job.
We are quiet, chew without taste or sound
Lest we disturb his tenuous weather.
He refills his drink again, Thunderbird or Ripple.
Night after night, we gauge the barometer, readying for the blow.

When my father died at 42 of cirrhosis I was glad
To be rid of him.
Forty years later, I still feel his landfall,
Yet now it is tempered with a realization—
My father, no matter who he was,
(never forgiving my mother's black eyes or brother's
bruises)—
Always
Brought his paycheck home to us
At the end of every week.

John Thompson

the dying kind

we regain our minds
like the dying kind
after having an autopsy

the mortician finds all the debris
and cleans the wounds
and lets you know
where the dying hides

inside you like a fetus
ready to claim
the embalming fluid
like warm milk

Sarah Thursday

Shard

I rub my bare feet into the carpet
searching for glass shards
this is what I do
because I don't want to be
caught off guard

and while glass does not belong in carpet
the callouses of my feet
will shed blood for it
open their cells like a curtain
like knifed butter

this is what I do
drag the palm of my hand
across the dresser top
to wipe off glass dust
run my hands under water
before I stop the army of red
droplets emerging

Sarah Thursday

I fought for love

aimed my spear high
body arched and focused eyes
but Love did not fight back
it opened its wide mouth
swallowed my weapons
and ground them into splinters
like shavings from his pencils

I laid myself at Love's feet
like a dog at a soldier's grave
clawing at fresh earth
hoping to unbury his memories
to dig out from soil words
he once wrote across my smile

I threw what stones I had left
to break Love's silence
but all the lines he drew
on the slope of my nose
were slowly rubbed away
like smudges of charcoal
he washed from his hands

K. Andrew Turner

Insomnia

Pinpricks
   like light that manifest
against the black

whispers air-heavy
     a chill
  and the cold smell
of snow

let this place breathe
  under
       water and let
me taste
         bliss

K. Andrew Turner

Time-less

Take
    breath into your lungs
s l o w

     as if a turtle
as if endless time

take breath

  let inspiration fill you
up from the bottom

rest
    in this weary world
energetic
       and deadly

you are not electric

simply flesh
     blood
  and pain

let it go
     breathe
s l o w
s l o w
s l o w e r

until you burst
       peace

K. Andrew Turner

Black

Black
   upon black
      upon black

the dark rainbow of clothes
easy to pick out
let me be
leave me alone
simple as can be
no thought

but it is more
 black is the word for fire
blanco like flame
a history
    and evolution of meaning
let it drape
 envelope and hold
let it drive the world back

simple
elegant
beautiful
ugly
all in one
      word
thought in
so many tongues

Susan Vannatta

I Miss the Flowers you Gave Me

Soft blue blooms
on the thin skin
beneath arms

Bright red bursts
of thumb tips
on collar bones

Warm yellow
like small sun stars
lighting up wrists

Deep purple pressed
like wine grapes
on a rib cage

Muted green irises
ringing around small
sea green eyes

A bouquet of color
and caring that faded
only when I didn't love them

enough

Susan Vannatta

Swallow

When you first said
her name
my mouth was California
in its drought
trying to drink up ocean water
to quench the cracking earth—
instead finding only salt
and sea snails drying in the sun.

I wanted to reach down
into your throat
with shaking hands
and spread my fingers out
to find the place
where the letters
and sounds swam
to gather them up
like fallen beads
from a torn string of pearls
in my palms—wet
with spit and clinging
as I pull desperately
at slipping syllables
trying to extract them from you.

Susan Vannatta

They are sand
sifting through and catching
on your oyster tongue
and I try to pick them up
grain by grain
before they are precious
stones again.

When I finally hold them—
dripping gems
freed from your chest—
all I can think
to do
is swallow
her name
whole.

Susan Vannatta

Bloom

You had a rose petal tongue
and thorns for teeth
I did not know
the bloom until you smiled

How to Go to Bed With Marilyn Monroe

After our 60th hour of the week working on a concrete machine
    shop floor
our women
seem so strange and far away they must be getting their hair dried
under a 3-eyed hairdresser's purple hairdryer
on Mars
getting to our women
would be as hard as driving back and forth across the L.A. basin
in rush-hour traffic
50 times
our fingertips so filthy
from black machine grease and dirty brown cutting oil and stinking
    green coolant
we'd have to take a shower for 3 days
before we could touch them
maybe
they are sitting on the stool at the corner of a bar smiling
at 3 horny sailors
or falling so far in love with a young handsome Hallmark Channel
    romantic movie actor
they will never want to look at us again
we have smelled the sour aftershave on the back of the neck of the
    machinist
on the next machine so long we can't remember
the scent of our woman's hair
the taste
of her lipstick

Fred Voss

as we pace in front of our machines beginning to know
how a man in Alcatraz felt
stuck on a rock for 30 years while his wife laughed drinking
    champagne going across
the Golden Gate bridge with a man giving her
orchid corsages
we are so tired
of the shapes of each other's asses
the length of each other's beards the way we spit into urinals as we piss
our shiny bald heads our grunting and sweating our scratching our
    armpits and asses
like apes our muscle car magazines our grip contests our "Hey Dude!"s
and "Wuzz Up?"s and fist knocks our bulging biceps and chest hairs
our women
are a drink of water to a man crawling across the Sahara Desert
dying of thirst
a hard-on
after 20 years of impotence
a reprieve
from the governor to a man who thought he was about to fry
in the electric chair
and when the quit-work whistle finally blows we race to our cars
and fire up the engines like we are all
about to fall into a honeymoon bed
with Marilyn Monroe.

Fred Voss

Steady as the Turning of the Earth

We are the machinists we know will stay at our machines
all our working days
there are the machinists who are only just passing through
this machine shop
something
in their eyes far far away they are already
playing blues harmonica in some Paris nightclub where the cool
    cats know their harmonica riffs
will live forever
or disappearing
never to return into some demonstration marching through the
    streets of downtown
L.A.
like Zapata
hopping onto his white horse ready to overturn everything
we are the lifer machinists
once we get our hands onto a good machine we never
let go
we wear trails
into the concrete floor around it with our bootheels
spurt machine grease onto the worm screws of our machine
like it was our religion
we have made a home
next to a drill and tap chart a toolbox full of tools
a steel workbench
worn shiny with our elbows we have memorized the jagged peaks
of the mountain range against the blue sky outside
a tin door

Fred Voss

know each chipped gear each cracked bearing by the rough rattling
        song it makes inside the head
of our machine
sip tea read books whistle tunes stare at war headlines dream of our
        woman's legs
beside the warm hum of our machine's motor
sad
for that alcoholic on the Bridgeport mill who's been sober for 5
        years but will soon end up
crawling skid row gutter again
or that hanging-by-a-thread engine lathe man with the worm scars
        across his wrist
who may any day end up back screaming
in the psyche ward
we are the lifers
bolted to this concrete floor like our machines
we may never quit to spread red and yellow oils across a canvas
like another Van Gogh
but as we lay the palms of our hands flat against the green sides of
        our machines we know
we are men and machines
steady as the turning
of the earth.

Fred Voss

Paycheck and Poem

Herman Melville's novel *White Jacket*
lying atop a tool steel box-end crescent wrench in my toolbox
my hand
on an Allen wrench turning set screw down tight
onto razor-sharp endmill so the endmill can cut steel
into manhole cover
my mind
rounding the tip of South America with Melville high up in the
    ship's crow's nest
wearing his white jacket freezing in a furious
Cape Horn wind
a thousand poems inside my head
a hundred shoulder bolts ¼-inch to 5/8-inch-in-diameter
in the tooling cabinet
behind me
I am literature and tapping fluid
James Joyce's *Ulysses* and *Machinery's Handbook*
Walt Whitman holding a glass of water to a dying Civil War
    soldier's lips
and a white Styrofoam cup of steaming-hot black coffee
in a hungover machinist's trembling fist
saw blade with my finger's blood dripping from its teeth
and Hemingway
with his knee blown apart limping for miles across a battlefield in Italy
the foreman
wanting the door hinges I'm carving right NOW
and Homer

Fred Voss

singing of Achilles swinging his mighty Trojan War sword
3,000 years ago
I am vise jaws
clamping onto a block of bronze so it can bring oxygen to a scuba
    diver's lungs
and Queequeg's freshly-carved coffin
popping
up out of the sea from Melville's sunken ship Pequod to float on the
    waves
so Ishmael can hug it
and survive
Hamlet
talking to a jester's skull in the bottom of a half-dug grave
and Ahmed
from Armenia with arthritic thumbs working on at age 77 heaving
    100-pound vises
onto his milling machine table so his granddaughter
can go to Princeton
a crow on a telephone wire outside this machine shop flapping its
    wings telling me
I'm stuck
on this machine
and Poe's raven perched outside his window croaking "Nevermore"
into his 3 am ear
I am muse and bolt
fable and rock-hard steel
foreman scream and Shelley ode
paycheck and poem.

Aruni Wijesinghe

Mating Season

tangle of wings and antennae
exposed in the midday heat
dust and the sighing of pines
caught off guard in a public display
mate with haste

four wings fold into one another
kaleidoscopes in, right sides facing
hide delicate branching patterns
from the harsh light of day

ignore the artificial shutter sounds
of iPhone camera's prying eyes
collapse in the sand, love-spent
only then flutter of wings give
glimpse of your true, beautiful selves,
fold again into secrets

"Are they fighting or fucking?"
all one and the same
in Mother Nature's brutal arena
we love, fight to the death

simultaneously Christian and lion
in lock- step, hip sway
and crush of mouth on mouth
fight-fuck while Romans
cheer from the Coliseum stands
and document the coupling
with ancient cameras

Aruni Wijesinghe

A Hymn to the Entering Year

"Not knowing when the dawn will come, I open every door."
—*Emily Dickinson*

I sofa the afternoon. Clouds cover the blue.
Clover girl, a fluted buttercup
I brush with my lips,
a dirge to the passing
of Spring.

       At times I feel *saudade*,
Portuguese strange in my mouth,
and grief presses me down against warm earth.
I am an empty cup left
on a picnic table outside Starbucks.
Waiting for you

       in the Hotel Galerias lobby,
now I ink our scars into a star map
on my right forearm.

The landscaper suggests we plant spreading lantana
across the sunbaked hillside, opt for bigger
citrus trees that will bear
fruit sooner.

Aruni Wijesinghe

        I ache with years and countless miles
on a stationary bike. A continent ablaze
half a world away and I knit
nests for homeless birds.

        The last orange grove
on Valencia Mesa is gone, but my senior year locker swings
open on quiet hinges.

        The decade flashes me
her blank calendar pages, legs under a short skirt.
The year winks, an engagement ring lost in the surf.

Scudding clouds pause over the burning plain.
Finches alight once more on unfamiliar branches.
The new day unfurls, a white flag.

Mariano Zaro

On a Silver Tray

The world has become heavy, I tell my doctor.
A door's handle, a page in a book,
an empty glass.

I want you to see this, she says.
She points at the black and white image
on her computer screen.

She wears a wedding band but I don't want to know
anything about her. I don't want her to have a husband,
children, parents, siblings.

This is your spine, she says. *From C-1 to L-5. Do you see these spots?*
Yes, I say. *What are they?*
Sadness, she says.

Are you sure? I ask.
It's a clear case, she says. *The location,*
the shape, the density.

Same patients present transparent sadness. We call it
Type Zero. Very difficult to diagnose, even using a dye for contrast.
Yours is translucent. Type 1.

And, it's shaped like pellets. You see? Very common in Type 1.
Type 2, the opaque sadness, is shaped like filaments that run
alongside the muscle fibers.

Mariano Zaro

Type 1 stays close to the spine. May cause weakness,
trembling, paresthesia, night sweats,
sexual dysfunction.

There is also Type 3. It's web-shaped, settles around the neck.
Patients describe it as having a bridle around the throat.
Produces speech impediments, sometimes muteness.

The last identified sadness is called Inner Type, she says.
It generates in the amygdala. It looks like a rain
of electrical spores that can reach any part of the body.

Does the Type 1 explain my symptoms? I ask.
We can't be sure, she says. *We are still in the early stages*
of research. But sadness explains many things.

What should I do? I ask.
Some patients try to rest more and calm down.
But sometimes they fall into hypersomnia, she says.

Balance is everything, she adds.
Some patients cry. Some play sports because of
dopamine release. Some listen to music. Bach, most of all.

I don't like sports, I say. *But I like Bach.*
What do you do with your own sadness, I ask.
I just keep plowing, she says.

183

Mariano Zaro

Will I improve? I ask.
You will, she says. *But there is no cure for sadness.*
It stays with you, always.

What about the future sadness? I ask.
We will cross that bridge when we get there.
Do you pray, meditate? she asks.

Not really, I say.
How can the body function with all this sadness? I ask.
Nobody knows, she says.

But some scientists theorize that the body wouldn't
be able to function without sadness.
Just a hypothesis.

Do you think we could survive
a lifelong load of sadness delivered in a single day? I ask.
She plays with her wedding band.

Imagine all your sadness, at once, on a silver tray, I say.
All at once, on a silver tray, she says, *like the head of John the Baptist.*

Mariano Zaro

Diagnosis of Men as They Undress

Some men undress and cover their chests—
arms folded like the front legs of a praying mantis.
The waistband of their underwear is flaccid but the socks
are tight and print deep grooves on their shins and ankles.
Fully naked they tilt their hips backward.
They bite their nails, they have sex with their eyes closed.
They infuse you with shy, post-orgasm sweat
that smells like malaise. They build roads, bridges.
It's customary for them to give you an expensive ring—
platinum, perhaps canary diamonds.
But the ring is always too big or too small.
You have to take it to the jewelry store to be resized.
The jeweler is clumsy, dents the metal;
and that's all you can see now when you put it on.

Some men undress and tilt their hips forward.
They also walk around with their arms slightly open,
as if their armpits were irritated, had a rash.
Many of them trim their pubic hair or shave it completely.
They like mirrors, towels, soap, body lotion, talcum powder.
When having sex, they become enthusiastic, acrobatic.
They show great willingness to please.
You almost want to give them a *Good job!* sticker,
an A+ on the report card, when they are finished.
One day they will hold your hand (guide your hand,
to be precise) and will tell you *Put your finger here, please.*

Mariano Zaro

Don't be prudish, do it—one, two fingers.
They will bury their faces in a pillow.
They will cry. They will be forever grateful.

Some men undress and when they remove their shirt
and leave it on a chair, for example,
the shirt becomes a fountain, then a lake.
They cannot see the lake or the fountain, just the shirt.
This gives them away, that's how you recognize them.
You can swim in the lake if you want, or cup your hands
and wash your face, drink if you are thirsty.
Sometimes they walk in the rain, alone, without hurry.
Talking with them for a while you cannot tell
if they are naked or fully clothed. Dogs lick their hands.
When they die, earth takes them in like lost children;
and you understand that they are going back home.
They don't leave much behind—a few coins, a pocket knife,
a white handkerchief with no initials—clean, neatly folded.

Matt Amott is a poet, musician and photographer who rambles around the Pacific Northwest. He is co-founder and co-editor of Six Ft. Swells Poetry Press and has been published in numerous collections as well as three books of his own, THE COAST IS CLEAR (Six Ft. Swells Press), GET WELL SOON and THE MEMORY OF HER (both by Epic Rites Press).

Mark James Andrews continues to live and write on the borderline of Detroit most of the time. His latest collection of poems is *Motor City is Burning & Other Rock & Roll Poems* from Gimmick Press. His poetry has most recently appeared in the anthology *RESPECT: The Poetry of Detroit Music* from Michigan State University Press.

Jason Baldinger is a poet from Pittsburgh, Pennsylvania. A former Writer in Residence at Osage Arts Community, he is co-founder and co-director of The Bridge Series. His books include *The Better Angels of our Nature, Everyone's Alone Tonight* with James Benger, and the chapbook *Blind Into Leaving*. His work has been published widely in print journals and online.

Luis Cuauhtémoc Berriozábal was born in Mexico, lives in Southern California, and works in the mental health field in Los Angeles, CA. His poetry has been published by Blue Collar Review, Kendra Steiner Editions, Mad Swirl, Nerve Cowboy, Pygmy Forest Press, The Journal of Heroin Love Songs, and ZYX.

A Best of the Net and Pushcart nominee, **Kelsey Bryan-Zwick** is a Spanish/English speaking poet. Author of *Watermarked* (Sadie Girl Press) Kelsey's poems appear in *petrichor, Cholla Needles*, and *Making Up*, an anthology by Picture Show Press. Writing towards her new collection, *Here Go the Knives*, find her at www.kelseybryanzwick.wixsite.com/poetry.

Ranney Campbell is a recovering journalist who currently builds walls out of boxes in semi-trailers at an Amazon warehouse like it's a virtual Tetris game (in the classical definition, of course) because she cannot speak Spanish, therefore, cannot get through the first round of cuts when applying at bail bonds.

Todd Cirillo is co-founder and editor of Six Ft. Swells Press. He is one of the originators of the After-Hours Poetry movement. He has many books and misdemeanors. His poems have appeared in numerous national and international literary journals, magazines and cocktails napkins everywhere. Todd lives in New Orleans, Louisiana where he seeks out shiny moments and strange wisdom.

Shutta Crum's poems have been published regularly since the 1970s. Her first chapbook *When You Get Here* is coming in 2020. She has several children's books written in verse, including THUNDER-BOOMER! (Clarion/HMH): a *Smithsonian Magazine Notable Book*, 2009, and an *American Library Assoc. Notable Book*. Her website is at: www.shutta.com.

John Dorsey is the author of several collections of poetry, including *Teaching the Dead to Sing: The Outlaw's Prayer, Sodomy is a City in New Jersey, Tombstone Factory, Appalachian Frankenstein, Being the Fire, Shoot the Messenger,* and *Your Daughter's Country*. He was the winner of the 2019 Terri Award given out at the Poetry Rendezvous.

John Drudge is a social worker in the field of disability management. He is the author of two books of poetry: March, and The Seasons of Us. His work appeared in *The Arlington Literary Journal, The Rye Whiskey Review, Poetica Review, The Alien Buddha Press, Montreal Writes, The Avocet, Black Coffee Review, The Ekphrastic Review,* and the *Adelaide Literary Magazine*. John lives in Caledon Ontario, Canada with his wife and two children.

James H Duncan is the editor of *Hobo Camp Review* and the author of *We Are All Terminal But This Exit Is Mine, Nights Without Rain, Vacancy, Feral Kingdom,* and other collections of poetry and fiction. He currently resides in upstate NY and reviews indie bookshops at www.jameshduncan.com.

Barbara Eknoian's work has appeared in Pearl, Chiron Review, Redshift, and Your Daily Poem. She has been twice-nominated for a Pushcart Prize. Her latest novel is *Hearts on Bergenline Avenue* available at Amazon. She lives with her extended family, son, daughter, and grandson, along with three dogs that she never picked out. People often comment that she's never lost her Jersey accent.

Alexis Rhone Fancher is published in *Best American Poetry, Rattle, Verse Daily, Duende, American Journal of Poetry, Wide Awake: Poets of Los Angeles*, and elsewhere. She's the author of five poetry collections, most recently *The Dead Kid Poems, (KYSO Flash Press, 2019).* A multiple Pushcart Prize nominee, Alexis is poetry editor of *Cultural Weekly.*

Scott Ferry helps our Veterans heal as a RN. His first collection, *The only thing that makes sense is to grow*, was published by Moon Tide in January 2020. You can follow him @ ferrypoetry.com.

Michael Flanagan was born in the Bronx, N.Y. Poems and stories of his have appeared in many small press periodicals across the country. His full-length collection, Days Like These, is now out from Luchador Press. You can find copies on sites such as Barnes & Noble and Amazon.

Bill Gainer is a storyteller, a humorist, an award-winning poet, and a maker of mysterious things. He is the publisher of the PEN Award winning R. L. Crow Publications and is the ongoing host of Red Alice's Poetry Emporium (Sacramento, CA). is latest book is *The Mysterious Book of old Man Poems.*

Tony Gloeggler is a life-long resident of New York City and has managed group homes for the mentally challenge for 40 years. His work has recently appeared in *Rattle, Poet Lore, Spillway, Chiron Review, & Nerve Cowboy.* His full length books include *One Wish Left* (Pavement Saw Press 2002), *Until The Last Light Leaves* (NYQ Books 2015). NYQ Books will publish his next book.

John Grey is an Australian poet, US resident. Recently published in *That, Dalhousie Review* and *North Dakota Quarterly* with work upcoming in *Qwerty, Chronogram* and *failbetter.*

John Grochalski is the author of the five poetry collections and two novels. Grochalski currently lives in Brooklyn, New York, where the garbage can smell like roses if you wish on it hard enough.

Michael D. Grover is a Florida born Poet that currently resides in Florida. His latest chapbook *Fuck Cancer Poems* is available on Blood Pudding Press. His new collection of Poems will soon be available from Cocklebur Press. Michael is the former Head Poetry Editor at Red Fez.

Stephanie Barbé Hammer is a 6 time Pushcart Prize nominee with work in the *Bellevue Literary Review, Pearl, Hayden's Ferry, Isthmus,* and the *Gold Man Review*. Stephanie was born in Manhattan and now wanders the woods of rural Washington State looking for a taco truck, a dry cleaner and someone to talk to.

Brian Harman was born and raised in Orange County, California, where he can be found trying new craft beers, creating themed music playlists, and rooting for the Angels. His work has been published in *Chiron Review, Nerve Cowboy, Misfit Magazine,* and elsewhere. His new book, *Suddenly, All Hell Broke Loose!!!* is available on Amazon and through Picture Show Press.

Curtis Hayes has worked in sawmills, greasy spoons, and as a grip, gaffer, and set builder in film productions. He's been a truck driver, a boat rigger, a print journalist and a screenwriter. His poetry has been featured in *Chiron Review, Trailer Park Quarterly, Cultural Weekly* and other small presses.

Steven Hendrix is the co-author of the poetry collection Leave With More Than You Came With from Arroyo Seco Press. He helped run the pop-up bookstore and reading series Read On Till Morning in San Pedro. He lives in San Francisco with his partner Erin and their son Langston.

Ted Jonathan is a poet and short story writer. Raised in the Bronx, he now lives in New Jersey. His collection of poems and short stories *Bones & Jokes* was published by NYQ Books (2009). His poetry collection *RUN* was published by NYQ Books (2016). He can be contacted at *theodorejon@yahoo.com*.

When not working on the poem **Robert Jay** works two jobs as a longshoreman and as a maintenance technician. His other random interests include Zen Buddhism, thunderstorms, Leftist political theory, Tai Chi, amateur photography, and weightlifting. He has been previously published in *Cadence Collective* and *For the Love of Words*.

Luke Kuzmish is a recovering addict, new father, newer husband, and software developer from Erie, Pennsylvania. His latest collection, "Hurry Up Wagon" was published by Poets' Hall Press in summer 2019.

Marie C Lecrivain is the editor of *poeticdiversity: the litzine of Los Angeles*. Her work has appeared in *Nonbinary Review, Orbis, Pirene's Fountain*, and others. She's the curator of several anthologies, including *Gondal Heights: A Bronte Tribute Anthology*.

Jennifer Lemming won 1st place for her poetry in the Dancing Poetry Contest in 2004. Her poems and short fiction have been published in online and print journals. Her latest chapbook, Star Slough, was published by Dark Heart Press, March 2019. She lives in Bismarck, North Dakota.

Cynthia Linville's work has appeared in many publications and several anthologies, and her two books of poems, *The Lost Thing and Out of Reach*, are available from Cold River Press. From 2008-2018, Linville served as Managing Editor of *Convergence: an online journal of poetry and art*.

John Macker's latest books are Atlas of Wolves (Stubborn Mule Press, 2019) and The Blues Drink Your Dreams Away: Selected Poems 1983-2018 (Stubborn Mule Press, 2018 and a finalist for a New Mexico/Arizona Book Award.) Macker has lived in Northern New Mexico for 24 years.

Tamara Madison is the author of the chapbook "The Belly Remembers", and two full-length volumes of poetry, "Wild Domestic" and "Moraine", all published by Pearl Editions. Her work has appeared in Chiron Review, Your Daily Poem, A Year of Being Here, Nerve Cowboy, the Writer's Almanac and other publications. She is thrilled to have recently retired from teaching English and French in a Los Angeles high school.

Betsy Mars was born in Connecticut. She spent two years in Brazil, where she attended kindergarten. Her father was a professor and her mother was a social worker, so she grew up to be a linguaphile, overly introspective, and a bleeding heart liberal. She loves to hang out with her adult children, friends and animals, travel, and write.

Daniel McGinn is a native Southern Californian. Daniel received his MFA in writing from Vermont College of Fine Arts at the age of 61 and his recent collection of poems, The Moon, My Lover, My Mother & The Dog, was published by Moon Tide Press.

Joan McNerney's poetry is found in many literary magazines such as *Seven Circle Press, Dinner with the Muse, Poet Warriors, Blueline,* and *Halcyon Days*. Her latest title, *The Muse In Miniature*, is available on Amazon.com and Cyberwit.net. She has four Best of the Net nominations.

Michael Minassian is a Contributing Editor for Verse-Virtual, an online magazine. His chapbooks include poetry: The Arboriculturist (2010); Chuncheon Journal (2019); and photography: Around the Bend (2017).

Robert A. Morris lives near Baton Rouge and works as a teacher. Besides poetry, he also writes fiction and bashes out the occasional song on his blue Stratocaster. A recent poem of his has been selected to appear in a future issue of As It Ought to Be Magazine. His work has appeared in The Main Street Rag, Reflect, and The Chaffin Review among others.

Robbi Nester is the author of 4 books, a chapbook, *Balance.* and three collections, *A Likely Story, Other-Wise,* and *Narrow Bridge*. She has also edited two anthologies, *The Liberal Media Made Me Do It!*, and an ekphrastic e-book, *Over the Moon: Birds, Beasts, and Trees*, which was published as a special issue of Poemeleon Poetry Journal.

Martina Reisz Newberry's newest collection is *Blues For French Roast With Chicory*. She is the author of nine books of poetry. Her work has been widely published in the U.S. and abroad. She lives in Los Angeles with her husband, Brian Newberry, a Media Creative.

Natalie Peterkin is an adjunct English Professor at East LA College and currently lives in Whittier, California. Her poetry often explores the themes of love, lust, and loss.

Rob Plath is most known for his monster poetry collection *A Bellyful of Anarchy*. He has published a shitload in the small presses. He lives in New York with his cat and tries his best to stay out of trouble.

Jeanette Powers is a working class non-binary anarchist artist and swimmer of rivers. They are currently traveling for 2020 on the Dandylion Riot tour, where they read poems and investigate alternative communal living spaces. They have been published widely and often with poetry and visual art, including one novel, Victimless Crime.

Wendy Rainey's poetry has been published or is forthcoming in *Trailer Park Quarterly, Nerve Cowboy, Chiron Review,* and several other journals and anthologies. Her book, *Hollywood Church: Short Stories and Poems,* was published by Vainglory Press in 2015. She is a contributing poetry editor on *Chiron Review.*

Tanya Rakh was born on the outskirts of time and space in a cardboard box. After extensive planet-hopping, she now lives in Madison, Wisconsin where she writes poetry and surrealist cross-genre amalgamations and edits manuscripts aplenty. Her first poetry collection, Hydrogen Sofi, is available now from Hammer & Anvil Books.

Gabriel Ricard writes, edits, and occasionally acts. His books Love and Quarters and Bondage Night are available through Moran Press, in addition to A Ludicrous Split (Alien Buddha Press) and Clouds of Hungry Dogs (Kleft Jaw Press). He is also a writer, performer, and producer with Belligerent Prom Queen Productions. He lives on Long Island.

Brian Rihlmann was born in New Jersey and currently resides in Reno, Nevada. He writes free verse poetry, and has been published in *The Blue Nib, The American Journal of Poetry, Cajun Mutt Press, The Rye Whiskey Review,* and others. His first poetry collection, *Ordinary Trauma,* (2019) was published by Alien Buddha Press.

Jason Ryberg is the author of thirteen books of poetry, six screenplays, a few short stories. He is currently an artist-in-residence at both The Prospero Institute of Disquieted P/o/e/t/i/c/s and the Osage Arts Community, and is an editor and designer at Spartan Books. His latest collection of poems is *Standing at the Intersection of Critical Mass and Event Horizon* (Luchador Press, 2019).

Alex Z. Salinas lives in San Antonio, Texas. His short fiction, poetry and op-eds have appeared in various print and electronic publications. He is the author of a full-length collection of poetry, WARBLES. He holds an M.A. in English Literature and Language from St. Mary's University.

Jeff Santosuosso is a business consultant and award-winning poet living in Pensacola, FL. His chap boo is Body of Water. He is Editor-in-Chief of *panoplyzine.com*. Jeff's work has appeared in *The Comstock Review, San Pedro River Review, South Florida Poetry Journal, Mojave Desert Review, The Lake (UK), Red Fez, First Literary Review-East, Texas Poetry Calendar, Avocet,* and other online and print publications.

Linda Singer has had three one act plays produced. She sold a script to Evening Shade and a joke to Readers Digest. Her poetry and short stories have been published in various journals. Linda cohost Poetry Apocalypse at Angeles Gate Cultural Center every third Sunday.

Jedediah Smith teaches literature, mythology, and composition at City College of San Francisco. Smith's recent work has appeared in *Chiron Review, California Quarterly, Mojave River Review,* and *American Journal of Poetry.*

Joan Jobe Smith, founding editor of PEARL (1974-2017) and Bukowski Review, rec'd her BA from CSULB and MFA from UCI; her work's appeared internationally in more than 1000 journals. Her recent poetry collection from NYQ Moonglow Á Go-Go is available on Amazon.

William Taylor Jr. is the author of numerous books of poetry, and a volume of fiction. His work has been published widely in journals across the globe, including *Rattle, The New York Quarterly,* and *The Chiron Review.* He was a recipient of the 2013 Kathy Acker Award. *Pretty Words to Say,* a new collection of poetry, is forthcoming from Six Ft. Swells Press.

Kareem Tayyar's most recent book is the poetry collection, *Immigrant Songs* (WordTech Editions, 2019), and he is a recipient of a 2019 Wurlitzer Poetry Fellowship.

Jeri Thompson is a poet, paying rent and writing in Long Beach, CA. BA in Creative Writing, CSULB, she studied under Elliott Fried and Gerald Locklin. Nominated for a Pushcart Prize in 2014, she's been published in; *Chiron Review, Carnival Lit Magazine, Silver Birch Press* (Silver, Green, and Summer), and *Anti Heroin Chic*. Soon to appear in Alien Buddha Press (April). Currently in Donna Hilbert's Tuesday night workshop, plotting her first chapbook.

Sarah Thursday, in addition to writing poetry, co-hosted 2nd Mondays Poetry Party, ran a poetry website called CadenceCollective.net, and founded Sadie Girl Press as a way to help publish local and emerging poets and artists. She has been published in many fine journals and anthologies, interviewed by Poetry LA, and received a 2017 Best of the Net nomination for "To the Men who told me my Love was not enough." Her poetry books are available at SadieGirlPress.com.

K. Andrew Turner writes queer, literary, and speculative prose and poetry. In 2013, he founded East Jasmine Review—an electronic literary journal. His full-length poetry collection *Heart, Mind, Blood, Skin* is now available from Finishing Line Press. He was a semifinalist for the 2016 Luminaire Award. You can find more at his website: www.kandrewturner.com

Susan Vannatta has been previously published in *The Left Coast Review*. Susan's first Chapbook, **Whiskey Letter**s, was published through Arroyo Seco Press. Susan uses her life as inspiration for her work, drawing off of the beauty that comes with inevitable pain. When she is not writing, she enjoys a good book, getting lost in her favorite shows, and cooking for as many people as will let her.

Fred Voss has published 3 full length collections of poetry with the U.K.'s Bloodaxe Books. He won the Port of Los Angeles/Long Beach Labor Coalition's 2016 Joe Hill Labor Poetry Award and has had featured programs on his poetry broadcast on National BBC Radio 4 in the U.K. and on WBAI Pacifica Radio New York.

Aruni Wijesinghe is a project manager, ESL teacher, occasional sous chef and erstwhile belly dance instructor. She is an emerging voice in LA and Orange County poetry and has performed her work around Southern California. She lives a quiet life with her husband Jeff and their cats Jack and Josie.

Mariano Zaro is the author of six books of poetry, most recently *Decoding Sparrows* (What Books, Los Angeles) and *Padre Tierra* (Olifante, Zaragoza, Spain). His poems are included in anthologies and literary journals in USA, Mexico and Spain. He has translated into Spanish American poets Tony Barnstone and Sholeh Wolpé.

Acknowledgements

Midnight In The Backyard of Lust and Longing was first published in Slipstream Summer 2019

She Says Stalker/He Says Fan was first published in The San Pedro River Review "Music" Issue. 2018

Daylight Savings was first published in The Ledge

Poet was first published in Nerve Cowboy

Every Broken Girl was Previously published in March 2018 online issue Anti Heroin Chic

My Father was previously published Summer 2015 issue Cadence Collective

The Boy Who Never Came of Age was previously published in Hiram Poetry Review

www.ingramcontent.com/pod-product-compliance
Lightning Source LLC
Chambersburg PA
CBHW071216090426

42736CB00014B/2843